Performing Commedia dell'Arte, 1570–1630

Performing Commedia dell'Arte, 1570–1630 explores the performance techniques employed in commedia dell'arte and the ways in which they served to rapidly spread the ideas that were to form the basis of modern theatre throughout Europe.

Chapters include one on why, what, and how actors improvised; one on acting styles, including dialects, voice and gesture; and one on masks and their uses and importance. These chapters on historical performance are followed by a coda on commedia dell'arte today. Together they offer readers a look at both past and present iterations of these performances.

Suitable for both scholars and performers, *Performing Commedia dell'Arte, 1570–1630* bears on essential questions about the techniques of performance and their utility for this important theatrical form.

Natalie Crohn Schmitt is Professor Emerita of Theatre and English at the University of Illinois, Chicago, USA. Her wide-ranging scholarship includes *Befriending the Commedia dell'Arte of Flaminio Scala: The Comic Scenarios* (2014) and essays on commedia dell'arte in *New Theatre Quarterly*, *Viator*, *Renaissance Drama*, and *Text and Performance Quarterly*. She is the recipient of two National Endowment for the Humanities fellowships and of Humanities Center fellowships at Stanford University and at the University of Illinois.

Performing Commedia dell'Arte, 1570–1630

Natalie Crohn Schmitt

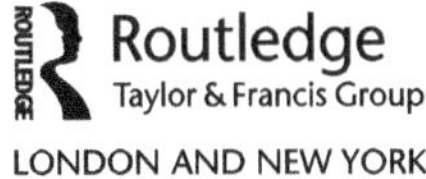

LONDON AND NEW YORK

First published 2020
by Routledge
2 Park Square, Milton Park, Abingdon, Oxon OX14 4RN

and by Routledge
52 Vanderbilt Avenue, New York, NY 10017

Routledge is an imprint of the Taylor & Francis Group, an informa business

First issued in paperback 2021

British Library Cataloguing-in-Publication Data
A catalogue record for this book is available from the British Library

Library of Congress Cataloging-in-Publication Data
A catalog record for this book has been requested

ISBN: 978-0-367-08565-0 (hbk)
ISBN: 978-1-03-208850-1 (pbk)
ISBN: 978-0-429-02304-0 (ebk)

Typeset in Times New Roman
by Apex CoVantage, LLC

Contents

Figures

Tables

Acknowledgments

Most of all, I would like to thank Joel Berman for his help throughout in ways big and small. I would also like to thank Sarah Bond for suggestions for images; Lucia Marchi for help with translation and especially for having called my attention to Emily Wilbourne's book; Hannah Hayes for her keen eye for details; and Jane Darcovich and Katherine Greenleaf for getting the photos right.

Introduction

"We can say that the commedia dell'arte has provided the basis for modern theatre in the Western world," asserts the Italianist Massimo Ciavolella (1992, p. 23). On the presumption of the veracity of this idea, this is a book about the means of performance – improvisation, acting style, and masks – that in large part enabled commedia dell'arte to become that basis, to show, insofar as the information can be recovered, what these performance techniques were, why they were used, and how they succeeded. A coda details some of the most successful uses of commedia dell'arte in performance today but disputes the idea that despite the enormous influence of commedia dell'arte in this century and in the last part of the twentieth century, there has been a continuous unbroken tradition that allows for its "authentic" performance.

For their own entertainment, in the early part of the sixteenth century Italian members of private men's learned societies wrote and performed plays, largely comedies, based on classical models. This *commedia erudite*, or learned drama, introduced classical form, character types, genres, and themes into the Renaissance. Although quite a number of these often rather stiff plays were published, it took the first professional players in Italy, the commedia dell'arte, beginning in the mid-sixteenth century, to call attention to, popularize, and disseminate this drama – from which they borrowed heavily. The overwhelming appeal of the professional players, first documented in Padua in 1545, was sardonically acknowledged as early as 1552 by a founding member of one of the learned societies in Florence. He noted of the commedia dell'arte that " 'their comedies have gained them all the glory and reputation:/ now the literati, beaten and outdone by the *zanni* (comic actors)/ can go hang themselves' " (translated and cited by Sampson, 2015, p. 188).[1] The itinerant players, regarded as unlettered by the literati, and looked down upon in the learned societies, had enlivened their performances with material from other sources: gags, the novella, and folk and street performance. And most notably, from the very beginning, the troupes of performers included women, the first professional actresses in Europe. Women contributed to the troupes' appeal (and opprobrium); but as, or more importantly for the theatre, their presence effected a reshaping and strengthening of women's roles and added the possibility of romance to the plots.

The seemingly endless iterations of and variations on the borrowed material and the addition of women performers proved compelling. Before long, the rapidly proliferating professional troupes, of varying quality, were performing, first in the streets and, in the case of the most successful ones, in the courts of Italy. They began to travel widely, eventually bringing their performances to the whole of the European continent, thus disseminating the material that became the basis for modern theatre.

On occasion the professional players performed scripted drama. But their considerable reputation, even to this day, comes from their having performed improvisationally and in masks. And while no single thing accounts for the success of the form – it lasted for over two hundred years – its success must be largely attributed to the means of its performance. These means were not unique in the early modern period, but the players took full advantage of them and made them famous.

In examination of the techniques of performance, I restrict myself to the sixty years, (1570-1630) during which time commedia dell'arte was thought to have been at its height, because any generalizations, given the long history of commedia dell'arte, otherwise become more difficult to make. The dates provided are certainly not determinate.

The borrowing and adapting of earlier materials for commedia dell'arte, particularly from the *commedia erudite*, has been examined by quite a few scholars, in English, especially by Richard Andrews (1993 and 2008) and Robert Henke (2002). The importance to the success of commedia dell'arte resulting from the use of the first professional women performers in modern Europe has been argued for by Rosalind Kerr (2014). I analyze the major contribution to commedia's success provided by its particular performance techniques.

A number of scholars have approached commedia dell'arte's means of performance and the nature of its effectiveness by the examination of a variety of sources, including the rich iconography of commedia dell'arte, techniques of predecessors, performance practices in other European countries, and even an Italian medical treatise. I focus more directly on commedia dell'arte's scenarios, essentially plot outlines and on the cultural context in which they were embedded.

The actors themselves said little about their means of performance, although their use continued throughout the existence of commedia. In the main, we have to turn to secondary sources. For improvisation, it is useful to see the larger context of its use in all the performing arts, including music, dance, storytelling, and oratory and to its use not only by actors, but also by preachers, mountebanks, and courtiers.

For its methods, we can turn to oratory about which there was a considerable literature. Particularly in the period under consideration, the most important aspect of commedia was speech; it was, in the main, a form of oratory. The examination of the methods of oratory make clear that in propagating their materials players were not "shamelessly pillaging" the materials of others, as theatre scholars continue to assert. Imitation and memory were understood as essential to improvisation.

An important extant primary source for learning about acting style are the scenarios. These specify character entrances and exits and the general nature of each scene, although sometimes frustratingly described in a kind of shorthand that must have been informative for the players but is not for us, e.g. "they have their antics." The only collection of commedia dell'arte scenarios to have been published in either the sixteenth or seventeenth centuries is that of the actor-manager Flaminio Scala, in 1611. Scenarios, almost throughout their history have been held in so little regard that, despite the fame of the commedia dell'arte, few of its roughly 750 extant scenarios had been published until this century. Scala's fifty scenarios, although unlike other scenarios in not presenting the difficulties for an editor of having to deal with them in manuscript form, much less in dialect, were published in a modern edition only in Italian in 1976, and thirty of them in a reliable English edition only in 2008. The Scala scenarios are special among extant scenarios because they were originally written and published with an eye to both readers and amateur performers and, on that account, contain more information than other scenarios. Among other things, they are a uniquely important primary source for information about the style of acting in commedia dell'arte performance. The wealth of descriptions of actions, motivations, and emotions in Scala's scenarios enable us to make good inferences about the particularly energetic and visual way in which the characters' emotions were conveyed. From these descriptions we can learn something about how commedia dell'arte was successfully disseminated.

Voice and gesture prove to be central to understanding how commedia dell'arte flourished both in Italy – where there was no common language and each character spoke in a distinct dialect – and throughout Europe where few knew any Italian dialect. Unlikely as it may seem, a useful source for the study of performance in the commedia dell'arte proves to be the classical author Quintilian. His writing on oratory and its uses of voice and gesture, was assiduously studied in the Latin grammar schools in the Renaissance throughout Europe. Emily Wilbourne's book on the origins of opera in commedia dell'arte (2014) invites new attention to the actors' use of voice as a means of bringing success to the commedia dell'arte.

Possible other sources for learning about acting style, particularly about gesture, are the iconography of the period, the works of Shakespeare, a contemporary of Scala's, a book published in 1600 by the dancing master, Fabritio Caroso, and an ambitious book by Giovanni Bonifaccio 1616, the intent of which was to document all of human gesture and more. Each of these has its limitations.

The Locatelli and Corsini collections of scenarios, containing many more tragicomedies and pastoral scenarios than the Scala collection, allow us to learn about personifications of allegorical figures, classical gods, devils and spirits, animals, and character masks (like Pantalone and Arlecchino) temporarily transformed into animals, trees, fountains, and stones. To learn about their masks, I work from the few scenarios from the Locatelli collection published in Italian and English in 1934 and from yet others published in Italian in 2007, and from the Corsini collection of one hundred scenarios published in both Italian and German in 2014. Almost no prior scholarly use has been made of either the Locatelli or Corsini collections, the only collections of scenarios that, like Scala's, are known to have come from commedia dell'arte's golden age. Of course, I also look at length at the character masks, which appear in most of the scenarios, regardless of genre. These have been very frequently described but their function has been insufficiently explored.

I show the many ways in which the particular performance techniques were not only practical but also allowed for the protected exploration of tensions otherwise below the level of consciousness or effectively suppressed, between social classes, men and women, young and old, and between foreign oppressors and the general populace. These techniques also allowed for the representation of deeply held beliefs about magic and astrology otherwise rigorously forbidden by the church. In ways that have hardly been recognized, the players' explorations resonated with their audiences, the members of which were experiencing rapidly changing social conditions.

Notes

1 More specifically, *zanni* refers to comic servants.

Works cited

Andrews, Richard. (1993). *Scripts and Scenarios: The Performance of Comedy in Renaissance Italy*. (Cambridge: Cambridge University Press).

Andrews, Richard, editor and translator. (2008). *The Commedia dell'Arte of Flaminio Scala: A Translation and Analysis of 30 Scenarios*. (Lanham, MD: Scarecrow Press).

Ciavolella, Massimo. (1992). "Text as (Pre) Text: *Erudite* Renaissance Comedy and the *Commedia Ridiculosa*. The Example of Gian Lorenzo Bernini's '*L'Impressario*'." *Rivista di studi italiani* 10: pp. 22–34.

Henke, Robert. (2002). *Performance and Literature in the Commedia Dell'Arte*. (Cambridge: Cambridge University Press).

Kerr, Rosalind. (2015). *The Rise of the Diva on the Sixteenth-Century Commedia dell'Arte Stage*. (Toronto, ON: University of Toronto Press).

Sampson, Lisa. (2015). "Amateurs Meet Professionals." In *The Reinvention of the Theatre in Sixteenth-Century Europe: Traditions, Text and Performances*, edited by T.F. Earle and Catarina Fouto. (London: Legenda).

Wilbourne, Emily. (2016). *Seventeenth-Century Opera and the Sound of the Commedia dell'Arte*. (Chicago, IL: The University of Chicago Press).

1 Improvisation

Why, what, how[1]

We need to understand commedia dell'arte improvisation within the context of Renaissance culture and its rhetorical tradition, a tradition that depended upon imitation and memory. Both imitation and memory were regarded not merely as skills of copying and reiteration but as arts of invention. Unlike earlier analyses of commedia dell'arte improvisation, this one calls attention to the centrality of these arts in the very process of improvisation. I look at why, what, and how commedia dell'arte actors improvised.

I limit my focus to the kind of improvisation that would most likely have been employed for the scenarios of Flaminio Scala (Scala, [1611], 1976).[2] This is a reasonable limitation. Theatre historian Louise George Clubb remarks that Scala's publication of his fifty scenarios in 1611 was "an event of the first importance to theatre history" because it gives a fuller idea of the nature of commedia dell'arte performance than any other single text has done (1995, pp. 128–129). Scala's collection represents commedia dell'arte at its height, 1570–1630. Recognizing its importance, others who have written on improvisation in commedia dell'arte, chiefly Tim Fitzpatrick (1995), Robert Henke (2002) and Quirino Galli (2005) have based their analyses on it as well.

Why did the actors improvise?

Although the principal fame of the commedia dell'arte (comedy of professional players) resulted from their playing *all'improvviso*, actors in troupes the caliber of those with which Scala had worked by 1611, among them the high-profile Desiosi, Uniti, and Accesi troupes, would also have acted in fully scripted plays in various genres.[3] They were clearly literate. A number of participants in the commedia dell'arte – Pier Maria Cecchini, Isabella Andreini, Adriano Valerini, and Flamino Scala – each wrote at least a single fully scripted play. Ironically, in the prologue to his scripted play, *Il finto marito*, 1619, Scala defended the art of improvisation.[4] Speaking as "The Player" he wrote, "Scala's invention has always been inspired, and that counts for everything in comedy" (Scala, 1976, p. cix-cx; cited in translation in Richards and Richards, 1990, p. 198). In other words, the precise words the actors spoke were not critical. Why did Scala, who, with that play, proved that he could write fully scripted plays, apparently prefer improvised comedy? Some of the possible answers to this question also suggest why the improvised comedy absorbed so much of the theatrical energy of the culture and was so long-lived and widespread.

Scholars have provided a variety of explanations for why the improvised form was used, probably most or all of them valid. Communication through scripted drama would have been impossible for traveling players because Italy was a peninsula without a unified national language and with very distinct dialects that were virtually separate languages. The poverty and instability of the companies together with the distinct dialects required of the various roles did not make writing for them an attractive prospect. The traveling players depended upon tailoring their performances to various and numerous performance locales and exigencies. Actors improvised so that their material could not so easily be used by competing troupes. Improvised drama avoided the inconvenience and disappointment that the time spent on premeditated drama so often occasioned. Improvised drama better enabled the performers to avoid censorship.

I offer yet another practical consideration. While we know that the memory of the actors was prodigious – Virginia Andreini learned a full-length musical role in six days, Vittoria Piissimi in a week (MacNeil, 2003, p. 13) – commedia dell'arte troupes, having stays in a single place for as long as three or four months, would have profited from being able to offer an even larger number of plays than they could commit to memory and this they could have done with improvised pieces.

There are, however, reasons for improvisation more compelling than the practical ones just listed, convincing though they may be. A number of the practical reasons provided presume that if circumstances had allowed the actors to perform fully scripted plays, they would have done so, but circumstances – censorship, cost, instability of the working conditions, competition, and the local dialects – did not allow it. No such presumption should be made.

Jeremy Lopez has pointed out that the success of the drama is fueled by its potential for failure: "The joy of the drama lies in the space for negotiation between success and failure" (2003, p. 134). When the drama is improvised, that sense of the potential for failure is enhanced. The outcome of improvisation is uncertain. The form seems open, the machinery of the plot fragile. The uncertainty specifically calls our attention to the improvising actor, not just to the material improvised. In that respect, the form is non-illusory. Other non-illusory conventions specifically in the commedia dell'arte – disguises, night scenes, the practical jokes (including bed-tricks) – are of a piece with the intrigue/improvisation in contributing to our sense that the action might fail. Despite our awareness that the trickster and lovers will prevail, the possibility that the performers and, consequently, the characters will not succeed adds to the excitement. The performance takes on the interest akin to that of a sporting event, especially because improvisation suggests that the performance is provided only for the audience at hand and is a one-time occurrence.

Richard Andrews notes that "an audience can find it amusing if characters are forced progressively to pile deceit upon deceit, just to sustain a plan that started as being simple" (1993, p. 79). This pleasure is greatly increased when the audience has the idea that it is not just the characters but the actors who are also trying to make their way through the obstacles of the improvised, or supposedly improvised, deceptions.

As defined by Stephen Greenblatt improvisation is the ability "to capitalize on the unforeseen and to transform given materials into one's own scenario. The spur-of-the-moment quality of improvisation is not as critical here as the opportunistic grasp of that which seems fixed and established" (Greenblatt, 2005, p. 27). The character's or the actor's ability or apparent ability to snatch the action from almost certain defeat is thrilling. When the character and actor do succeed in overcoming the hurdles, they seem to share in the pleasure of the play. The actor and the audience become complicit in the pleasure of putting on the play. The relationship between the audience and actors, then, despite the fact that some of the actors are masked, is closer than in scripted theatre.[5]

In commedia dell'arte, the asides, the visual takes of the figures at the windows and the parallels in the action, most noticeably in the double-plotting, all contribute to the audience's double perception, the greatest of which is of both the actor and the role. This duality not only gives the audience a feeling of superiority to the clearly created characters, it keeps it very busy, leading it to believe that the action is more complicated and faster than it is, hence more exciting and funnier.

One can understand then why the improvising commedia dell'arte performers exaggerated the distance between what they called "premeditated" drama and their own playing "*all'improvviso*." They downplayed the importance of the scenario, of memorization, and of rehearsal to increase the audience's appreciation of their skills and to increase the sense of the danger and uniqueness of the occasion.[6]

Improvisation not only has its own particular theatrical interest, it was also consistent more largely with cultural values and practice of the time. The audience's heightened consciousness of both the improvising actor and her role is of a piece with the preoccupation in the late sixteenth century with the discrepancy and interplay between reality and appearance, with what Michael Shapiro calls the "dual consciousness" of reality and illusion" (1977, pp. 104–105).

In the culture at large, great respect was given to oral skills including the art of quick and biting repartee. Making a good impression in Renaissance society required that one be a good speaker. Thus, one might compliment a new father by telling him that his son would grow up to be a *bel parlatore* (fine speaker). A father might advise "his sons to read history, short stories and jest books to find epigrams which 'may bring you honour in a conversation'" (Burke, 1987 p. 97, 81). Castiglione's *The Book of the Courtier* stresses grace and the avoidance of affectation, in speech above all. The chief characteristic of the courtier was *sprezzatura*: a seemingly easy grace and effortlessness in speaking and acting (Castiglione, 1986, pp. xxvi-xxviii). Greenblatt calls this kind of improvisation "self-fashioning" and points to the extent to which it was "a central mode of Renaissance behavior" (2005, p. 229). In a culture where every word was part of a performance, speech and its accompanying gestures were of crucial importance in the presentation of self (Burke, 1987, p. 8).[7] From the beginning, a grammar school education, dominated by the teaching of rhetoric, stressed the need for improvisation, for ad-lib quickness and the coaxing of chance, the need for improvisation (Lanham, 1976, p. 2). The all-important source, Quintilian, asserted that for orators "the greatest fruit of our studies, the richest harvest of our long labours is the power of improvisation" (Quintilian [95 CE], 2001, vol. IV, p. 373). In the literary academies members not only provided orations but also improvised on a theme about which they had not been told beforehand (Henke, 2002, p. 41). In the Accademia Fiorentina, orations in the vernacular in the 1540s were regularly open to the public including artisans and shopkeepers who would otherwise also have been familiar with such improvisation from the pulpit, the law, and street performance (Bryce, 1995, p. 83).

While *sprezzatura* was the desired skill of the courtier and orators, underclass rogues relied on the same linguistic prowess and social dexterity. They too lived by their verbal craft and wit (Henke, 1997, p. 7). In the culture at large, according to cultural historian Peter Burke, "formal oral performances were frequent and excited much interest. . . . Most of these performances – songs, stories, plays, sermons, speeches, the sales-talk of charlatans, and so on – were improvised, or more exactly, semi – improvised" (Burke, 1985, p. 81). Verbal games were also popular. Cultural historian Guido Ruggiero notes the great and expanding interest in play in fifteenth and sixteenth-century Italy. Books of the period, often reprinted, served as guides to such play, usually quick and witty word play, tactfully competitive storytelling, or argumentation (Ruggiero, 2007, p. 43.[8] While the play described in these books was intended for an evening's gathering of aristocrats, it is well to remember the extent to which people of all classes passed their leisure time together with songs, stories, and jokes. They entertained themselves with improvised or semi-improvised performances.

Musicologist Howard Mayer Brown tells us that sixteenth- and seventeenth-century musicians could improvise polyphonic music extemporaneously. They could also improvise embellishments to their own taste on some music that had already been composed (Brown, 1976, p. xx). *Cantatore improvviso* (improvisational singer) was a profession (Burke, 1987, pp. 81, 97). Dance historian Julia Sutton observes that the two closely related principles of improvisation and semi-improvisation (variation) are also evident in the Italian dance manuals of the same period. She describes how a courtly dancer first learned the basic steps and patterns and after that the many variations that could be used at appropriate moments while still keeping to the general structure of the music and the dance. She also finds evidence of some free improvisation within the set dances (Sutton, 1995, pp. 27–28).[9] Thus both musicians and dancers, if their skill were sufficient, could improvise. In short, there was a context for the appreciation of the actor who could improvise and of actors who could improvise together, skillfully.

What was the nature of the improvisation?

Having enumerated practical reasons for improvisation as well as those having to do with its general theatrical interest and particular cultural circumstances, I address questions about the nature of commedia dell'arte improvisation. In this section and the next, my analysis differs from the ones on the nature of the improvisation provided by Tim Fitzpatrick in his *Relationship of Oral and Literate Performance Process in the Commedia dell'Arte: Beyond the Improvisation/Memorisation Divide* (1995), and by Robert Henke in his *Performance and Literature in the Commedia Dell'Arte* (2002) in my focus on the centrality of imitation and memory in the very process of improvisation.

Fitzpatrick reaches his conclusions without taking account of the rhetorical context and incorrectly presumes a logical divide between improvisation and memory. Nonetheless, extrapolating from the research of Milman Parry ([1928] 1971) and Albert Lord ([1960] 2000) on storytelling in other times and cultures, in general, Fitzpatrick infers correctly, I believe, the kinds of processes employed by commedia dell'arte performers. Henke, basing his analysis on the work of Walter J. Ong's well-known distinction between "residual orality" and literacy, enhances the work of Fitzpatrick by making use of the rhetorical context.[10] While both Fitzpatrick and Henke premise their work on antitheses I question, I do not disagree with the primary findings of either. I expand upon the work of both by setting the improvisational means more securely in its rhetorical and cultural context.

The information available from the time of Scala is primarily about verbal rather than physical improvisation. So, like Fitzpatrick, and Henke, I focus my remarks on verbal improvisation in the commedia dell'arte. Consistent with the very high regard in which verbal skills were held, commedia dell'arte improvisation, in its golden age, was, on the evidence of the Scala scenarios, primarily a verbal art. Stephen Orgel reminds us that the terms "auditory" and "audience" both refer to sound and that "theatre in 1605 was assumed to be a verbal medium" (Orgel, [1976] 2014, pp. 16–17)

The performers did not improvise freely but rather within a limited framework. Indeed, Francesco Andreini, in his introduction to the Scala scenarios, tells us that Scala provided everything but the words the actors spoke (in Scala [1611] 1976, p. 12). The actors improvised upon what was, in most instances in Scala, a carefully constructed scenario. Further, improvisation was delimited (and facilitated) by actors playing a single role, often for life, by the scenarios' repetitions of the same bourgeois domestic conflicts, and by avoidance of religion, politics, and commerce, and, by the absence, for the most part, of children, mothers, peasants, and aristocrats. Because actors rehearsed, and repeated performances of a scenario, they likely fell into familiar patterns.

Much of the dialogue in Scala's complex scenarios had to have been taken up with establishing the relationships, the history leading up to the events shown (provided in the argument, the "*Argumento*," preceding each scenario),[11] the explanation of desired ends, the obstacles to achieving them, the intended actions, and their often unintended outcomes. Further, the plot complexities within the acts often required summations of the action up to that point, for which Scala indicates specific insertion points. The scenarios and each of the scenes within them served as a structure and within that the actors would have had to make structures for the development of the action in the scene, including the order in which the information was to be provided.

At the same time, the verbal cannot be seen as separate from the physical. Theatre historian David Wiles remarks that acting seen from below on raised stages (like those of the commedia dell'arte) inevitably calls attention to the body [and its actions] since the spectators' heads are close to the actors' legs (Wiles, 2003, p. 118). Actions specified in Scala's scenarios include quite vulgar ones for his lower-class characters: fondling, vomiting, the emptying of a chamber pot onto characters below, and attempted defecation and castration. The strong physical dimension to the performance, including in the many *lazzi* (gags, primarily physical), chase scenes, threated duels, and the use of many stage properties, is beyond question. The masks for the *parti ridicule* (comic roles) practically necessitated physical acting. Yet ironically, by limiting facial expressions, masks intensified the audiences' focus on the words (Wiles, 2007, 128, 132). Apart from the visual interest of the actions, actions would have served to greatly clarify these words, particularly because of the actors' use of different dialects for the various characters. In Chapter 2, I direct my attention to the importance of the physical in relation to the verbal improvisation.

That verbal improvisation was through and through influenced by the written word. In his meticulously documented study, Henke argues that professional improvising actors brought literary materials and modalities into stage composition even at its most basic levels (Henke, 2002, pp. 107, 195). In this, it seems, the professional actors were not alone. Historian Adam Fox, in his study, *Oral and Literate Culture in England, 1500–1700*, argues that, while each culture must be examined on a case by case basis, he is impressed by the extent to which the oral traditions, long before 1500 were indebted to the written word, either directly or through innumerable intermediaries, to a far deeper level in society and in much greater quantity than people have supposed. "No one was immune from the influences wrought by the written word. Everyone who spoke the language, uttered its habitual sayings, sang its popular songs, inherited its commonplace assumptions and adhered to its normative beliefs, was absorbed in a world governed by text." Fox cautions against the idea that writing necessarily destroys memory and undermines oral tradition. The growth of literacy and the spread of print did not destroy or weaken the force of communication by word of mouth. " 'Oral' and 'literate' are rarely discrete entities or inversely related. Instead they form a dynamic continuum, each feeding in and out of the other to the development and nourishment of both" (Fox, 2000, pp. 10, 50; see also pp. 410, 242, 363, 413).[12] Fox's argument is important for me in that it suggests that ideas in rhetoric about the nature of invention and the importance of memory in improvisation were not restricted to those who were schooled.

Historian of Italian education, Paul Grendler, tends to confirm Fox's view that literacy or the effect of literacy was more widespread and earlier than many have assumed. He even entertains the idea that in the high Renaissance in Italy (1450–1527) functional literacy existed among a broad spectrum of the male population. And Latin, he says, exerted an enormous influence in culture and society not only through the grammar schools, conducted in Latin, and, to a lesser extent, through the vernacular schools, that, oddly enough, used primers either in Latin or primarily in Latin, but also through the church, the government, and the law (Grendler, 1989, pp. 47, 149, 152).

The actor's improvisation, both verbal and physical, like the invention in the scenario, was imitative. The root word of "invention," "*invenire*," means to "come upon" or "to find." For rhetorical man, and I include the Renaissance orator, preacher, mountebank, courtier, and actor, what we think of as a natural verbal spontaneity was never allowed to develop. Rhetoric entailed language, spoken or written, that was preplanned (Lanham, 1976, p. 3). While its invention was not spontaneous, neither was it imitative as we understand the word now – an exact copy of the original. Verbatim repetition was not highly respected, nor was mere paraphrase (Greene, 1982, p. 31). In fact, for the rhetorician, simply memorizing *ad verbum* (word for word) and then speaking what he had memorized was a mark of ineptitude (Carruthers, 2008, p. 256). Petrarch (1304-1374) whose work was widely disseminated in the period, explained that a proper imitator should take care that what he writes resembles the original without reproducing it: "The resemblance should not be that of a portrait to the sitter – in that case the closer the likeness the better – but it should be the resemblance of a son to his father" (cited in Greene, 1982, p. 95).[13] The imitation should be creative. Authentic imitation consisted of conversion or transposition of the source material. Imitation was the source of invention (Greene, 1982, pp. 31, 38).

The school libraries of the Renaissance consisted primarily of collections of proverbs, maxims, apothegms, fables, examples, similes, descriptions, and selected quotations from authors like Cicero, Plutarch, Aristotle, and Seneca. Volumes of these sayings were often grouped under commonplace headings like adversity, anger, envy, fear, God, honesty, justice, prudence, revenge, and truth so that schoolboys could readily gather them to enhance their oral and written compositions (Crane, 1964, pp. 31, 34).

Actors, orators, preachers, poets, and playwrights proceeded in the same manner of composition as schoolboys. In 1634, the actor and playwright Niccolò Barbieri, describing the process of improvising actors, explained that "there is no good book that they have not read, or fine conceit that they have not gathered, or description left unimitated or choice remark unappropriated, for they read wisely and deflower books. Many provide themselves with translated discourses from other languages" (cited in Lea, [1934] 1962, pp. 104). Similarly, the character Ricciolina, alone on stage in one of Domenico Bruni's prologues 1621, complains about the incessant demands made on her:

> Hey Ricciolina, bring me the Lover's part from *Fiammetta*, I want to study it. Pantalone wants the letters of Calmo. The Capitano needs the *Bravure* of Captain Spavento. Zanni needs Bertoldo's *Astuzie*, the *Fugilozio* and the *Hours of Recreation*. Graziano needs the *Sentenzie dell'Erborente* and the *Novissima Poliantea*, while Franceschina wants a copy of *Celestina* so that she can learn how to play the bawd. The Lover wants the works of Plato, and they're all asking me for this and that at the same time!
>
> (cited in Fitzpatrick, 1995, p. 22, note 2)

While schoolboys were not expected to be able to use the materials creatively, orators, like bees, Petrarch said, should "not [be] storing up the flowers but turning them into honey, thus making one thing of many various ones, but different and better." Bees otherwise "would have no credit" (cited in Greene, 1982, pp. 98–99).[14] Likewise, Quintilian, esteemed in the Renaissance, was known to have scorned orators who simply repeated the words of others *verbatim* as much as he scorned those who appeared to be reciting a memorized speech word for word (Carruthers, 2008, pp. 272–273). The trained orator could speak without appearing to have memorized at all. He relied heavily on his memory of many sources but was to recreate the source material in words that were at least partly his own. The admired skill lay in being able to call up these sources at will and adapt them to the occasion, to revise, change, digress and add, without giving any indication of having relied on prepared and rehearsed material at all.

Henke observes that there are insertion points in the Scala scenarios for particular kinds of set pieces, for instance, about love, love betrayed, or faithless children (Henke, 2002, p. 120).[15] They would not have been quite that, of course. They would have to have been accommodated to the particular situations in the scenarios and perhaps to the particular audience. More than that, the actors would have been expected to make the source material into something that was their own and perhaps new each time. For Petrarch it was a point of pride to eliminate all repetitions even of his own words (cited in Greene, 1982, p. 19). Rehearsals and repeated performances of the same scenario would probably have diminished the amount of new creation but the recycled speeches and dialogues may have been unstable nonetheless, depending on the actor, and on her energy that day. In that sense the actors would have been improvising even largely set speeches and dialogues.

Sprezzatura, the easy grace of the courtier, belied the deliberate effort, craft, and craftiness involved.

> To labour at what one is doing and, as we say, to make bones over it, shows an extreme lack of grace, and causes everything, whatever its worth, to be discounted. . . . The most important thing is to conceal . . . [one's art], because if it is revealed, this discredits a man completely and ruins his reputation.
>
> (Castiglione, [1528] 1976, p. 67)

Castiglione echoes Quintilian who similarly stressed that the artlessness of impromptu speaking was the product of extensive preparation. In the same vein, Cecchini, 1628, reminds those who play the lovers that "they should be continually reading literature to acquire that habit of pleasing expression which deceives the hearer into supposing that it springs from the natural wit of the speaker (cited in Lea, 1934, 1962, p. 104). Rosalind Kerr provides examples of the way the celebrated *innamorata* Isabella Andreini could devise verse that deliberately intermixed lines from Petrarch or interpolated a line of his composition after every second line of her own. Thus she intentionally called attention to the adroitness with which she manipulated her source material. For those members of the audience who knew their Petrarch, she amplified and enriched her relationship with them (Kerr, 2006, p. 89). Such invention was to have seemed effortless.

To make evident the work that went into improvisation, including extensive practice, rehearsal, and the effort of memorization would have diminished the sense of the performance's immediacy, of its being a work that was performed only for the audience at hand. It would have diminished the audience's admiration for the performer as an improviser. Quintilian even suggests various means of heightening the sense that the speech was improvised, like pausing and seeming to grope for a word (Quintilian [c. 95 CE] 2001, vol. V, p. 83) and thus increasing the audience's sense that the speaker might fail.

Much of the speech in the scenarios seems to have been copious. Erasmus, in his very influential *De utraque verborum ac rerum copia*, 1512, declares at the onset "The speech of man is a magnificent and impressive thing when it surges along like a golden river, with thoughts and words pouring out in rich abundance" (Rhodes, 1992, p. 46). Copiousness was greatly facilitated by memorization; the well-versed speaker was never at a loss for words.

The much admired "copiousness," however, was not simply fluency or abundant style but, as Thomas Sloane neatly explains, "having wherewithal at the ready," "fecundity, resourcefulness, and quickness" (1997, pp. 56, 76). Everything was to be glossed – greetings and farewells, ordinary transactions, cowardly capitulations, simple meals. Famously, in commedia dell'arte, even the eating of a fly was made to sparkle.

Although the action of the scenarios rarely turns on the captain, this character appears in thirty-six of the forty scenarios in the collection that Scala identifies as comic. He is present, in large part, to boast, threaten duels, and capitulate. In Francesco Andreini's publication of the boasts of Captain Spavento, prompted by his servant Trappola, boasts run to four and five pages in length (Andreini, [1607] 1987). Andreini, who played the role of the captain as Captain Spavento probably elaborated upon them for publication. If he did so, he makes clear that part of what the audience enjoyed was their very verbosity. Similarly, the doctor was full of talk and the lovers could wax poetic at length.

While the actor's improvisation was within the restricted range of the character he played and the repeated situations that character encountered, at the same time it required considerable range and flexibility. In the Scala scenarios, characters are required to silently make clear that they recognize someone in disguise, declare passionate love, weep freely (as men could do without shame), rage in fury, in jealousy vow revenge, duel to protect their honor – often all in quick succession.

How did the actors improvise?

Memoria (memory) was the psychological faculty valued above all others from late antiquity through the Renaissance (Carruthers, 2008, p. 9).[16] Throughout the Renaissance, even for those who were literate, reading and writing did not supplant memory; indeed the book often served as a way to remember a text (Carruthers, 2008, p. 9). Oral performances relied upon memory. "Invention" was dependent upon having an "inventory" of material from which to work (the two words share the same Latin root) (Carruthers, 1993, pp. 11–12). Mary Carruthers explains that the goal in employing the techniques of memorization was not to give students all the information they might be asked to repeat on an examination but to give orators the means and material to invent their material, both beforehand and, most importantly, as they were speaking (1993, p. 9). The orator was to have absorbed the material so that he could speak from his storehouse of memorized material without appearing to have memorized at all, to have transformed the material into his own. Writing about universities, which he characterizes as "a verbal arena," Paul F. Grendler observes that the highly valued spontaneous teaching was dependant on a capacious memory.[17] The malapropisms of the commedia dell'arte character Dr. Graziano make clear that he had not digested or even understood what he had memorized. He revealed his art, such as it was, and so discredited himself.[18] He did not have the educated *memoria* of the trained orator.

Memoria, like imitation, "is most usefully thought of as a compositional art" (Carruthers, 2003, p. 9).[19] It was the compositional process that brought together in one piece the separate bits filed and cross-filed in the places of one's memory. The result was the *res*, that is, the model of the composition that the orator or preacher would recall when preparing to speak. The orator might write out and memorize some of his speech (perhaps the beginning) and work to perfect particular phrases but working from the *res* allowed him to make use of momentary chances and sudden inspiration (Carruthers, 2008, pp. 244, 254). The valuing of *memoria* did not change for many centuries after printed material became available. Despite the availability of books, Carruthers (2008) believes that memory remained central because of the identity of memory with creative thinking, invention, recollection, and the ability to make judgments (pp. 9, 195).[20]

Cicero, in his definitions of the five parts of rhetoric in *De inventione*, (Cicero [c. 91–88 BCE], 1949, 2000) and the unknown author of *Rhetorica ad Herennium*, thought in the Renaissance to have been Cicero, made the distinction between two kinds of "artificial" or studied memory: *memoria verborum* (verbatim memorization) and *memoria rerum* (the remembering of substance, that is to say, subject matters, the main words in a quotation, the main topics of an argument, the gist of a story, or the like).[21] The distinction was well-known and traditional (Carruthers, 2008, p. 91).[22] Because *memoria rerum* involves an adaptation of the original material for compositional purposes rather than its complete iteration, it was preferred to rote iteration, especially in composition, even when the speaker had accurate command of the original words (Carruthers, 2008, pp. 93, 234–235).

Memoria rerum is also the faster of the two memorization techniques and allows one to suit the words to the occasion and not risk forgetting a word or forgetting altogether what one is saying (Carruthers, 2008, p. 111). In the case of dialogue, it also keeps one from being thrown off by a fellow actor using different words or indeed adding a new idea. It is the kind of memory actors would have required to learn the particulars of each scenario and the development of each scene. This is not to say that commedia dell'arte actors did not employ rote memory as well.

Cecchini cautions that the words immediately following the delivery of a memorized speech "shall fit uniformly with what was premeditated so that the theft may appear as birthright and not rapine" (Lea, 1934, p. 104). One wonders whether Cecchini's language reflects the strong moral emphasis that Cicero, Quintilian, and Augustine gave to rhetoric. The memory for things, *memoria rerum*, compels the recollector to actively shape material for an occasion. It is thus regarded as ethically more valuable than *memoria verborum* (Carruthers, 2008, pp. 14, 93). Knowledge that gets absorbed shows up as habits of reasoning, speaking, writing, and imagining.

One of the fundamental principles of memory is to "divide" the material to be remembered into small units. Breaking up the material into small manageable units is what neuropsychologists now call "chunking." While each chunk is divisible into further chunks and each into further subsets, the number of items in each set that can be remembered is between five and nine (Carruthers, 2008, p. 105).[23] As a practice recommended by Quintilian, and known as *divisio*, chunking was well-known in the Renaissance (Carruthers, 2008, pp. 8, 105, 109). *Rhetorica ad Herennium*, one of the most widely taught texts on rhetoric in the grammar schools, itself serves as a model of such division. For example:

> The Division we shall make is the following: we shall set forth the things we intend to praise or censure; then recount the events, observing their precise sequence and chronology, so that one may understand what the person under discussion did and with what prudence and caution. The following is the order we must keep when portraying a life: (1) External Circumstances: [and then praise or censure of the man relative to these in order]. (2) Next we must pass to the Physical Advantages [and to praise or censure of him in relation to these in order]. Then we shall return to External circumstances and consider his virtues and defects of Character evinced with respect to these . . . [in order].
>
> ([Cicero] ([80s, 90s BCE], 1954, pp. 178–181)

The Scala scenario itself, as Henke observes, serves to divide the action into interactional units or speech acts that allowed actors to organize and compartmentalize their speeches in the topical manner of the Renaissance rhetorician (Henke, 2002, p. 43).

The effective speaker keyed these units into some rigid, easily recalled order (Carruthers, 2008, p. 8). Recommended techniques for memorizing the sequence of the divided material included memorable schematic images, including, places, verbal/visual puns, grids, or alphabetical, numerical, or key word orders.[24] That is, the effective speaker "inventoried" his relevant memory store, or "inventory." The individual's own system for doing so was regarded as preferable to any preset one (Carruthers, 2008, p. 136).[25] Quintilian recommended that for a speech one should always keep in mind the *modus* or "way" and the *finis* or "goal." If one did so he could digress without losing his way or forgetting how much he had yet to cover (Carruthers, 2008, p. 109). For the overall structure of each of the scenes themselves, the Scala scenario provides the way and the goal.

Once one had set up the system of mental *notations* for each of the sections, he could confidently access each at random without having to go back to the beginning each time or, worse, try to remember something unsystematically. Carruthers points out that the ability to replicate memorized material again and again, forwards and backwards, and in all sorts of combinations remained a revered skill at least until the end of the Renaissance. The point was not that the orator had learned the material by rote but that he knew the material so well that he could revise, change, digress, and add with freedom and confidence during the delivery itself (Carruthers, 2008, pp. 8, 21). Thus Petrarch wrote that he had so thoroughly "absorbed and fixed" Virgil, Horace, Livy, and Cicero that, "not only in my memory but in my very marrow, these have become so much a part of myself, that even though I should never read them again they would cling in my spirit, deep-rooted in its inmost recesses" (Petrarch 23,19, cited in Greene, 1982, p. 99).[26] With her role in the very marrow of her bones, the improvising actor could vary her set speeches and address anew any of the recurring or even fresh situations she encountered in the scenarios.

How did the actors improvise together?

Thus far, I have considered improvisation or invention as a solo activity, but the Scala scenarios consist preponderantly of dialogues rather than monologues. Actors improvised together. While in one sense improvising with others is more difficult, it is also easier in that actors can play off one another. Close listening can be a rich source for invention.

Lodovico Zorzi stated that he believed it impossible for three people to improvise together (Zorzi, 1983, p. 72). Taking his cue from Zorzi, Fitzpatrick argues that three-way scenes in Scala, at any given moment, can be reduced to two-way scenes, with two characters siding together. Fitzpatrick further argues that the large number of scenes, averaging forty-five per scenario, and entrances and exits with a deliberate minimization of the number of characters involved in the action at any one time are designed to achieve a simplification "of the action and (more importantly) of the interaction between characters." He goes so far as to call the small number of characters on stage at any one time, averaging three, as "Scala's principal dramaturgical invention" (Fitzpatrick, 1995, p. 107).

A count of scenes and characters in a random selection of six plays of the earlier written comedy, the *commedia erudita*, shows that the number of scenes in the commedia dell'arte was not significantly different from in the fully scripted plays. Nor does the average number of characters per scene appear to be significantly different (Table 1.1). It seems that Scala simply followed convention in these matters.

Table 1.1 Plays: number of scenes and number of speaking characters.

Play	*No. of scenes*	*Speaking characters*
Bernardo Dovizi da Bibbiena, *La calandria* (The Comedy of Calandro), 1513.	59	2.2
Pietro Aretino, *Il marescalco* (The Master of the Horse), 1533	54	2.7
Alessandro Piccolomini, *L'alessandro* (Alessandro), 1543	26	2.8
Annibal Caro, *Gli straccioni* (The Scruffy Scoundrels), 1544	25	3.3
Giovan Maria Cecchi, *L'assiuolo* (The Horned Owl), 1549	32	2.3
Girolamo Bargagli, *La pellegrina* (The Female Pilgrim), 1564-68	38	2.3

Further, it is not clear to me that the scenes in Scala's scenarios are restricted to two-way interactions. Just to take one of the scenarios, Day 25, *La gelosa Isabella*, the scenes at 1, 7; 1, 14–17; 2, 18; and 3, 4 provide opportunity for three points of view to be expressed in a three-way scene.[27] I elaborate on only the first of these scenes, 1, 7:

> ISABELLA again at the window, tells Orazio to go to the maidservant and not make her wait any longer. Capitano asks Isabella what is the matter with her; she tells him she has been betrayed and cut to the quick. Capitano blusters; Orazio and Flavio draw [their swords] against him, and, fighting, they go up the street; Isabella at the window [at this point the next scene begins].

Isabella is distraught, believing that Orazio is no longer faithful to her but rather favors the maidservant. When she explains to the Captain that she has been betrayed, the Captain, immediately infatuated with Isabella, vaingloriously vows to come to her defense against the treacherous villain. Orazio, now challenged, and feeling that both his relationship with Isabella and his honor are imperiled, draws his sword on the Captain. His loyal friend Flavio does likewise. Orazio and Flavio speak in concert but the Captain and Isabella each have separate roles to play. It is possible that Isabella ceases to interact verbally in the scene after she explains to the Captain that she has been wronged. It would be far more interesting, however, if Isabella continued to have her say. And why could she not?

Unquestionably, two people can improvise together more easily than any larger number. However, the work of the approximately thirty-five improvisational groups performing in any given week in my hometown, Chicago – despite the fact that almost all of their work relies on spontaneous improvisation that would have been alien to the Renaissance – serves to call into question some assumptions that have gained currency about the limitations inherent to improvisation.[28] On occasion, I have observed scenes by Chicago improv groups in which as many as seven people interact at one time, each representing independent points of view. And these groups, unlike the commedia dell'arte performers, are not working from fixed characters in familiar situations in rehearsed scenes. Charna Halpern, co-founder in 1981 of the influential Chicago improv training school and performance venue, I.O. and its continuing director, comments that it is no more difficult for a number of actors to improvise together than it is for them to engage in conversation at a dinner party.[29] Groups of Chicago actors improvising in performance can also perform in unison, including in song with improvised lyrics relevant to the scene at hand, complete with improvised single instrument musical accompaniment.[30]

It is likely that in the Renaissance some things other than any limitations inherent to improvisation mostly kept the number of viewpoints being expressed on stage at any one time to two. The majority of scenes in the Italian Renaissance plays and scenarios consist either of alternating conceits or of thrust and parry, the structure of debate. This structure has had a long life in drama; it is present in scenes of plays by Ibsen, O'Neill, and Pinter, for instance. The PBS NewsHour regularly features Mark Shields, Democrat and David Brooks, Republican, who until the election of US President Donald Trump in 2016, could be counted on to represent two opposing views. In *On the Contrary*, Thomas Sloane notes that "oral combat remained an essential feature of grammar school instruction even on the lowest levels, or forms ." Sloane, even in his book title, makes the case that the essence of Ciceronian rhetoric is such argumentation: "*inventio* is dialogic and it must be pursued pro and con" (Sloane, 1997, pp. 32, 76). Richard Lanham (1976), in synthesizing the various techniques of teaching rhetoric in the Renaissance, includes: teach the "doctrine of antilogy, the ability to argue with equal skill on either side of a question" (p. 2). Not surprisingly dialogue, scenes, and even whole plays are two-sided arguments. Several of Scala's scenarios in effect dramatize a debate on the question "which is more important, friendship or love?" or "which is more important, romantic love or filial obedience?"

The action depends upon secrets and misunderstandings, which in turn depend upon there being few characters present. As Henke has observed the scenes generally represent a single action. That is a common, even a defining characteristic of a dramatic scene and undoubtedly did make improvisation more focused. The many scenes in both the *commedia erudita* and the commedia dell'arte keep the action moving as speedily as comedy generally requires, keep the multiple plots up in the air, rapidly change the mood from scene to scene, and provide a sense of the vitality of the street life in the cities. Thus, when the total number of characters in the scenario might well be no more than ten, there are many advantages to a sequence of short scene with few characters.

Blocking on stage does not appear to have been a significant one of them. The example of Chicago improvisation, like commedia dell'arte, performed in a small space on a fixed set, shows the ease with which many actors together can block themselves. In the commedia dell'arte, movement on stage was facilitated by the ever present piazza setting with its two or three houses with windows and doors that directed focus and with which the actors became very familiar, by the status relationships of the characters, and by variations in movement determined by specified entrances, actions, and exits, and by character.

Certain movement patterns characterized each of the commedia dell'arte characters. Women were not free to move about the streets and, to establish this in the Scala scenarios, they often appear first only at the window (Tylus, 1997). When

Scala then takes the dramatic liberty of having them come out into the street, the women may be in disguise or they stay close to the house and do not greatly move about. Pedrolino, on the other hand, often takes charge of the action and his movement about the stage would have made that clear. Captain Spavento, in his boasts, would also have taken stage. Henke points to the fact that the large group scenes that often concluded the play would have been organized by predictable and constant spatial configurations based on status relationships and would not need to have been rehearsed (Henke, 2002, p. 14).

Perhaps the observations that have been made about improvisation between actors in the commedia dell'arte are best subsumed under the guiding principle of I.O.'s training in improvisation in Chicago: "yes, &." (Halpern, Close, and Johnson, 1994, pp. 94, 97). The I.O. actors are taught to go along with whatever the actors with whom they are working have established. Charna Halpern urges actors to listen carefully for "the game" of the scene established through that agreement, usually in the first three interchanges: "Find your game, and you've found your scene" (Halpern, Close, and Johnson, 1994, p. 46). Of course, in Scala, the game is pre-established by the scenario: "they speak at cross-purposes," for instance.

Kathleen Lea (1934, 1962) suggested that "all the speeches of the *commedia dell'arte* are built upon a collapsible principle, they could be protracted or cut short to meet any emergency" (p. 23). Richard Andrews expands upon this idea to include dialogue, in what he terms the "elastic gag." He comments that "probably a third character would need to interrupt . . . [the improvising actors] before they ran out of material" (Andrews, and, p. 133). Henke believes that the beginning and ending points of the elastic gag were, in fact, predetermined, but that what came in between could contract or expand according to the actor's will and the audience's pleasure (2002, p. 34). Consistent with Halpern's observation about the "game," of the scene, Andrews observes that "in this 'elastic' kind of structure, an element of mirror imaging or echoing is common, because whoever speaks or acts second can take the tone, rhythm or style from the item which came first."[31] Halpern's concept of "the game" allows for the expansion of the ideas of Lea and Andrews to include, for instance, loving exchanges between lovers, as well as speeches and gags.

******

I have argued that actors can improvise together with facility even in groups, that commedia dell'arte improvised drama has unique compelling interests particularly in the culture and rhetorical tradition in which it flourished and in which improvisation played a central part, and that imitation and memory were critical to it. Richard Andrews points outs that Siro Ferrone and others have insisted that commedia dell'arte was practiced in a theatrical culture where the term "plagiarism" had no negative connotations, and perhaps where the concept did not even exist. Nonetheless, Andrews describes the Scala material as "often unscrupulously pillaged" (Andrews, 2008, p. xxxv). In this chapter, I have maintained that not only did imitation and memorization have no negative connotations, they were respected as essential arts of invention.

Notes

1 This chapter, with a few additions, originally appeared as an essay in *Renaissance Drama*, new series 38 (2010), pp. 225-249. Reprinted with the permission of the University of Chicago Press.
2 In addition to the 1976 Marotti edition in Italian, thirty of the scenarios are available in English (Scala, 2008), and all fifty are available in English in a rather unreliable translation by Henry Salerno, (Scala, [1967] 1989) frequently republished in paperback because of its abiding use by actors).
3 By 1614 Scala managed the prestigious troupe *I confidenti* then under the patronage of Don Giovanni de' Medici. So his reputation as a *capocomico* before that date had to have been considerable.
4 The play is closely modeled on Scala's scenario *Il marito.*
5 Using the word "*psyche*" in its Greek sense to imply the presence of a living spirit, David Wiles argues further that masks served to "repsychologise" rather than "depsychologise" the face . . . bringing the character closer to the audience as well" (Wiles, 2007, p. 132).
6 Thus Evaristo Gherardi, who played Arlecchino at the Comédie Italienne for many years, wrote in his introduction to his collection of scripts in French in 1700: "Italian comedians learn nothing by heart, and . . . in playing comedy, it is enough for them to have seen the subject of it only a moment before going on the stage." (Gherardi, [1700] 1970, p. 58).
7 "The rhetorical view of life . . . begins with the centrality of language. It conceives reality as fundamentally dramatic, man as fundamentally a role player" (Lanham, 1976, p. 4). Small wonder that the distinction between reality and appearance was problematic.
8 George W. McClure notes women's games that challenged them to impersonate all manner of learned, prestigious, or controversial professionals and to debate a wide range of topics concerning such arts. He points to Innocenzio Ringhieri's long popular *Cento giuochi liberali et d'ingegno* (*One Hundred Games of Learning and Wit*) published in Bologna in 1551, 1553, 1555, and 1580, and especially to the twenty-six topoi or "*quesiti*" that Ringhieri appended revealing the range of intellectual and social issues surrounding the professions and how such subjects might be appropriate for polite female debate (McClure, 2004, p. 54). For upper-class parlor games for mixed company see Girolamo Bargagli, *Dialogo de'giuochi che nelle vegghie Sanesi si usano di fare: Del materiale Intronato,* published in Siena in 1572, and in Venice in 1574, 1575, 1581, 1591, 1592, 1598, and 1609. Both Ringhieri and Bargagli are available in recent editions. McClure, chapter 2, provides a rich account of jokes, carnival songs, and verbal games of the period.
9 Whether such improvisation took place in Italian Renaissance folk dance, Sutton cannot ascertain because there are no written records of folk dance from the period. She does note that throughout Western dance history there has been cross-fertilization between cultivated and folk dance and that some of the same dances appear today in folk dance that appear in the Reniassance courtly dance manuals (Sutton, 1995, p. 29).
10 For Ong's use of his idea of "residual orality" see, for instance, Walter J. Ong (1965, pp. 145–154). Ong's *Orality and Literacy: The Technologizing of the Word* (1982) has been translated into eleven languages.
11 Within the scenario, Scala sometimes specifies the points at which potential performers are to include the relevant information supplied in the argument and readers are to imagine its being provided. Scala's are the only extant scenarios to include arguments. Prior to the publication of the scenarios, I presume that Scala, as *capocomico,* provided the antefact to the performers orally.
12 Ong saw orality and literacy as binaries with a cognitive revolution following from the advent of literacy. In contradistinction to this "strong theory," Fox's argument

is consistent with the "weak theory" originally presented by Ruth Finnegan (1988). Finnegan emphasizes the coexistence and interaction of orality and literacy coupled with a more modest, non-determinist view of literacy as a facilitator of cognitive change (pp. 141, 160). For a tidy summary of the argument against Ong, see Joyce Coleman (1996, pp 1–33). See *The Book of Memory* for Carruthers' brusque dismissal of the distinction between oral and written style in medieval sermons (2008, p. 260).

13 For the popularity of Petrarch and Petrarchism see Kerr (2006, pp. 71–92).

14 The analogy to mellification, from Seneca the younger, Epistle 84, 65 AD, was widespread. Another frequent analogy was to digestion.

15 Already in 1976, Edward Leon Sostek in his unpublished dissertation claimed, in Chapter 3, "Identification of Prepared Materials and Scenario Cues," that there were set speeches and insertion points for them in Scala.

16 The title, *The Book of Memory,* suits Carruthers' argument that literacy did not replace memory. Erasmus wrote in 1512, "I have never approved of youths writing down every word they hear, for this practice leads them to neglect the cultivation of memory, allowing for the fact that some may want to make a few brief notes of certain things, but that only until such time as the memory has been strengthened and they no longer desire the prop of the written word" (Erasmus, (*[1512*] 1978, p. 690).

17 The conferring of a doctorate was based solely on an oral performance for which the candidate was given at most twenty-four hours in which to prepare to expound authoritatively on several assigned randomly selected passages in various texts, and then to respond to the examiners' counter-arguments (Grendler, 2002, pp. 152, 175).

18 Paul Grendler observes that learning as it was employed was mocked, even by some few educated, as irrelevant, trivial, and pedantic. And the ideas, texts, and institutions that were authorities on learning were condemned as irrelevant to reality and civic life (Grendler, 1969, pp. 148, 161). On the linguistic stew, *macaronic verba,* of lawyers, see Burke (1987, pp. 85, 87).

19 Carruthers points out that the pioneering and influential Frances Yates examined memory only as a means to repeat previously stored material (Carruthers, 2003, p. 9; Yates, 1966). In defining the rhetorical use of memory as simply "the techniques for memorizing a speech as well as making it memorable for an audience," Henke also overlooks its critical importance to invention (Henke, 2002, p. 42).

20 It was thought that a person having no memory, if such a person could be, would be without moral character (Carruthers, 2008, p. 14).

21 To make this distinction clear, Yates uses the Hubbell translation of Cicero but, more literally, adds the words "*res*" ("things") and "*verba*" (Yates, 1966, pp. 8–9).

22 Grendler believes that it is not possible to overestimate the importance of these two works as cultural and literary models (Grendler, 1989, p. 216).

23 Her source is Dudai (2002). See Dudai: "Capacity," pp. 31–33; "Internal Representation" pp. 133–135; and "Working Memory," pp. 249–250.

24 Peter of Ravenna (1448) claimed to have memorized twenty thousand legal extracts, one thousand texts from Ovid, two hundred from Cicero, three hundred sayings of the philosophers, the greater part of Valerius Maximus, and seven thousand texts from scripture and more, in a mental system based on the letters of the alphabet (Carruthers, 2008, p. 143).

25 *Rhetorica ad Herennium* provides an example of a single pictorial image for memorizing *ad rerum* the chief issues involved in a law case in which the prosecutor has said that the defendant killed a man by poison, charged that the motive was an inheritance, and declared that there are many witnesses and accessories to this act ([Cicero] ([80s, 90s BCE], 1954, pp. 214–215). Carruthers makes the point, however, that many important visual images that serve memory are not pictorial (Carruthers, 2008, p. 21).

26 In English, to know something "backwards and forwards" still means to have fully absorbed it.

27 M.A. Katritzky's observations on the presence of the actress in visual representations of mountebank performance lead her to argue that "actresses gave the commedia dell'arte its defining nucleus, which is to be sought not in the servant-master duo promoted by traditional scholarship, but in the characteristic Zanni-Pantalone-*Innamorata* trio." (Katritzky, 2007, p. 215). Her argument is based on pictorial evidence, so she does not address the nature of their interaction.

28 Second City, Chicago's best-known improv group, has performed here since the 1950s, but uses improvisation primarily in rehearsal rather than in performance and thus differs from the many other groups in the city that engage in fully spontaneous improvised performances up to an hour and a half in length.

29 E-mail to author July 18, 2008. Halpern has also taught improvisation for groups of rank amateurs at CERN, British Petroleum, and Abbott Laboratories. Until Halpern's training school and performance center I.O. was threatened with legal action by the Olympic committee, it was called the "ImprovOlympic," reflecting in its name, as does the name of another Chicago group, "ComedySportz," the close relationship between improvisation and sport.

30 Their practice defies Virginia Scott's assertion that "an actor cannot, of course, improvise to music" (Scott, 1990, p. 65).

31 Andrews comments that Moliere must have observed a particular rhythmic structure, which was adopted by improvising actors in their playing of the "elastic gag." Seeing that it had a theatrical validity in its own right, Moliere used it in his scripts, but his dialogue, unlike that of the improvising actors, is so apt that it does not allow for any elasticity (Andrews, 1993, p. 185). However, skilled actors, particularly with the repetition provided by rehearsal and performance can also find the exact timing and there is no reason to believe they would have departed from it. Actors in Second City, which generally uses improvisation in rehearsal but not in performance, have demonstrated this skill.

Works cited

Andreini, Francesco. ([1611] 1976). "Cortesi lettori." In Flaminio Scala, *Il teatro delle favole rappresentative*, edited by Ferruccio Marotti. (Milano: II Polifilo).

Andreini, Francesco. ([1607] 1987). *Le bravura del capitano Spavento*. Edited by Roberto Tessari. (Pisa: Giardini).

Andrews, Richard. (1993). *Scripts and Scenarios: The Performance of Comedy in Renaissance Italy*. (Cambridge: Cambridge University Press).

Andrews, Richard. (2005). "Shakespeare and Italian Comedy." In *Shakespeare and Renaissance Europe*, edited by Andrew Hadfield and Paul Hammond, pp. 123–149. (London: Arden Shakespeare).

Brown, Howard Mayer. (1976). *Embellishing Sixteenth-Century Music*. (Oxford: Oxford University Press).

Bryce, Judith. (1995). "The Oral World of the Early Accademia Fiorentina." *Renaissance Studies* 9 (1): pp. 77–103.

Burke, Peter. ([1987], 2005). *The Historical Anthropology of Early Modern Italy: Essays on Perception and Communication*. (Cambridge: Cambridge University Press).

Carruthers, Mary. (1993). "The Poet as Master Builder: Composition and Locational Memory in the Middle Ages." *New Literary History* 24 (4): pp. 881–904.

Carruthers, Mary. (2003). *The Craft of Thought: Meditation, Rhetoric, and the Making of Images, 400–1200*. (Cambridge: Cambridge University Press).

Carruthers, Mary. (2008). *The Book of Memory, A Study of Memory in Medieval Culture*. (Cambridge: Cambridge University Press).

Castiglione, Baldessar. ([1528] 1976). *The Book of the Courtier*. Translated by George Bull. (Middlesex, UK: Penguin Books).

Cicero, M. Tullius. ([c. 91–88 BCE], 1949, 2000). *On Invention*. Translated by H.M. Hubbell. (Cambridge, MA: Harvard University Press).

[Cicero, M. Tullius]. ([c. 80s, 90s BCE] 1954). *Rhetorica ad Herennium*. Translated by Harry Caplan. (Cambridge, MA: Harvard University Press).

Clubb, Louise George. (1995). "Italian Renaissance Theatre." In *Oxford Illustrated History of Theatre*, edited by John Russell Brown, pp. 107–141. (Oxford: Oxford University Press).

Coleman, Joyce. (1996). *Public Reading and the Reading Public in Late Medieval England and France*. (Cambridge: Cambridge University Press).

Crane, William G. (1964). *Wit and Rhetoric in the Renaissance: The Formal Basis of Elizabethan Prose Style*. (Gloucester, MA: Peter Smith).

Dudai, Yadin. (2002). *Memory from A to Z: Keywords, Concepts, and Beyond*. (Oxford: Oxford University Press).

Erasmus, Desiderius. ([1512] 1978). *Collected Works of Erasmus: Literary and Educational Writings, 2, De copia/De ratione studii*. Edited by Craig R. Thompson. (Toronto, ON: University of Toronto Press).

Finnegan, Ruth. (1988). *Literacy and Orality: Studies in the Technology of Communication*. (Oxford: Blackwell).

Fitzpatrick, Tim. (1995). *The Relationship of Oral and Literate Performance Processes in the Commedia dell'Arte: Beyond the Improvisation/Memorisation Divide*. (Lewiston, NY: Edwin Mellen Press).

Fox, Adam. (2000). *Oral and Literate Culture in England 1500–1700*. (Oxford: Oxford University Press).

Galli, Quirino. (2005). *Gli scenario di Flaminio Scala: Lingua e teoria teatrale*. (Salerno: Pietro Laveglia).

Gherardi, Evaristo. ([1700] 1970). "On the Art of Italian Comedians" Preface to *Le théâtre italien de Gherardi*, 1700. In *Actors on Acting: The Theories, Techniques, and Practices of the Great Actors of All Times as Told in Their Own Words*, edited by Toby Cole and Helen Krich Chinoy, p. 58. (New York: Crown).

Greenblatt, Stephen. (2005). *Renaissance Self-fashioning from More to Shakespeare*. (Chicago, IL: University of Chicago Press).

Greene, Thomas M. (1982). *The Light in Troy: Imitation and Discovery in Renaissance Poetry*. (New Haven, CT: Yale University Press).

Grendler, Paul F. (1969). *Critics of the Italian World: 1530–1560, Anton Francesco Doni, Nicolò Franco & Ortensio Lando*. (Madison: University of Wisconsin Press).

Grendler, Paul F. (1989). *Schooling in Renaissance Italy: Literacy and Learning, 1300–1600*. (Baltimore, MD: Johns Hopkins University Press).

Grendler, Paul. (2002). *The Universities of the Italian Renaissance*. (Baltimore, MD: Johns Hopkins University Press).

Halpern, Charna, Del Close, and Kim "Howard" Johnson. (1994). *Truth in Comedy: The Manual of Improvisation*. (Colorado Springs, CO: Meriwether).

Henke, Robert. (1997). "The Italian Mountebank and the *Commedia dell'Arte*." *Theatre Survey* 38 (2): pp. 1–29.

Henke, Robert. (2002). *Performance and Literature in the Commedia Dell'Arte*. (Cambridge: Cambridge University Press).

Katritzky, M.A. (2007). *Women, Medicine, and Theatre, 1500–1750: Literary Mountebanks and Quacks*. (Aldershot, England: Ashgate).

Kerr, Rosalind. (2006). "Isabella Andreini (Comica Gelosa 1560–1604): Petrarchism for the Theatre Public." *Quaderni d'Italianistica* 27 (2): pp. 71–92.

Lanham, Richard A. (1976). *The Motives of Eloquence: Literary Rhetoric in the Renaissance*. (New Haven, CT: Yale University Press).

Lea, K.M. ([1934], 1962). *Italian Popular Comedy: A Study in the Commedia Dell'Arte, 1560–1620*, (2 vols). (Oxford: Clarendon Press).

Lopez, Jeremy. (2003). *Theatrical Convention and Audience Response in Early Modern Drama*. (Cambridge: Cambridge University Press).

Lord, Alfred. ([1968] 2000). *The Singer of Tales*. (New York: Athenaeum).

MacNeil, Anne. (2003). *Music and Women of the Commedia dell'Arte in the Late Sixteenth Century*. (Oxford: Oxford University Press).

McClure, George W. (2004). *The Culture of Profession in Late Renaissance Italy*. (Toronto, ON: University of Toronto Press).

Ong, Walter J. (1965). "Oral Residue in Tudor Prose Style." *PMLA* 80 (3): pp. 145–154.

Ong, Walter J. (1982). *Orality and Literacy: The Technologizing of the Word*. (London: Methuen).

Orgel, Stephen. ([1975] 2014). "Theatre and Audiences." In *European Theatre Performance Practice 1580–1750*, edited by Robert Henke and M.A. Katritzky. (Burlington, VT: Ashgate).

Parry, Milman. ([1928] 1971). *The Making of Homeric Verse: The Collected Papers of Milman Parry*. Edited and translated by Adam Parry. (Oxford: Clarendon).

Quintilian, M. Fabius. ([c. 90 AD] 2001). *The Orator's Education [Institutio oratoria]*. Edited and translated by Donald A. Russell. (5 vols). (Cambridge, MA: Harvard University Press).

Rhodes, Neil. (1992). *The Power of Eloquence and English Renaissance Literature*. (New York: St Martin's Press).

Richards, Kenneth and Laura Richards. (1990). *The Commedia dell'Arte: A Documentary History*. (Oxford: Basil Blackwell).

Ruggiero, Guido. (2007). *Machiavelli in Love: Sex, Self, and Society in the Italian Renaissance*. (Baltimore, MD: Johns Hopkins University Press).

Scala, Flaminio. (1611*). Il teatro delle favole rappresentative, overo La rricrecatione comica, boscareccia, e tragica: Divisa in cinquanta giornate* (Venice: Battista Pulciani).

Scala, Flaminio. ([1967] 1989). *Scenarios of the commedia dell'arte: Flaminio Scala's Il teatro delle favole rappresentativa*. Edited and translated by Salerno, Henry F. (New York: Limelight).

Scala, Flaminio. ([1611] 1976). *Il teatro delle favole rappresentative*. (2 vols). Edited by Ferruccio Marotti. (Milano: Il Polifilo).

Scala, Flaminio. ([1619] 1990). "Prologue to *Il finto marito*." In *The Commedia dell'Arte: A Documentary History*, edited by Kenneth Richards and Laura Richards, p. 198. (Oxford: Basil Blackwell).

Scala, Flaminio. (2008). *The Commedia dell'Arte of Flaminio Scala: A Translation and Analysis of 30 Scenarios*. Edited and Translated by Richard Andrews. (Plymouth, UK, Scarecrow).

Schmitt, Natalie Crohn. (2010). "Improvisation in the Commedia dell'Arte in its Golden Age: Why, What, How." In *Renaissance Drama*, new series 38, pp. 225–249.

Scott, Virginia. (1990). *The Commedia dell'Arte in Paris 1644–1697*. (Charlottesville: University of Virginia Press).

Shapiro, Michael. (1977). *Children of the Revels*. (New York: Columbia University Press).

Sloane, Thomas O. (1997). *On the Contrary: The Protocol of Traditional Rhetoric*. (Washington, DC: Catholic University of America Press).

Sostek, Edward Leon. (1976). "The *Commedia dell'Arte*: A Study in Dramatic Form." PhD. Dissertation. University of Iowa.

Sutton, Julia. (1995). *Courtly Dance of the Renaissance: A New Translation and edition of Fabritio Caroso, Nobiltà di Dame (1600)*. Music transcribed and edited by F. Marian Walker. (Mineola, NY: Dover Publications).

Tylus, Jane. (1997). "Women at the Windows: *Commedia dell'Arte* and Theatrical Practice in Early Modern Italy." *Theatre Journal* 49: pp. 323–342.

Wiles, David. (2003). *A Short History of Western Performance Space*. (Cambridge: Cambridge University Press).

Wiles, David. (2007). *Mask and Performance in Greek Tragedy: From Ancient Festival to Modern Experimentation*. (Cambridge: Cambridge University Press).

Yates, Frances. (1966). *The Art of Memory*. (Chicago, IL: University of Chicago Press).

Zorzi, Lodovico. (1983). "Intorno alla commedia dell'arte." In *Arte della maschera della commedia dell'arte*, edited by Donato Sartori and Bruno Lanata, pp. 63–83. (Florence: Usher).

2 Acting styles

Dialects, voice, gesture

I attend to what we can know about the uses of dialect, the sound of speech, and gesture in commedia dell'arte for the period 1570–1630. Finally, I turn to the scenarios of Flaminio Scala, originally published in 1611 to see what we can learn from them about performance, more particularly, about gesture.[1]

Dialects

The extant speeches and dialogues from the commedia dell'arte of the period make clear that it was a very verbal art, closely related to the art of rhetoric and to the earlier written comedy. The language could be rich in imagery, full of puns and wit, and, depending on the particular character, could include Petrarchean-like love poetry, pedantry and malapropisms, rants, and braggadocio full of classical references. Speeches could be long.[2] Yet each of the characters spoke in a distinct regional dialect. Pantalone spoke in a Venetian dialect, the doctor in Bolognese, the lovers in Tuscan, the *zanni* (servants) spoke a rural Bergamesque from the Alpine valley above Bergamo, and the captain usually spoke a kind of Spanish-Italian in we do not know what dialect – in the case of Francesco Andreini, Tuscan. Various critics have tried to understand why the characters spoke in different dialects, how actors understood one another speaking them, and how audiences understood the actors.[3]

For the traveling players it is not clear what the reasonable alternative to all these dialects might have been because Italy was not unified until 1860, and even after that for a long time many people did not speak the then official language, literary Tuscan. Except in the universities and the Latin grammar schools, and in the Mass, during the sixteenth and seventeenth centuries, "all social classes in Italy, regardless of wealth or education, spoke dialect at all times"(Clivio, 1989, p. 228).[4] There is no one dialect that players traveling to various parts of Italy might have used and been understood. The problem of comprehension for the audience had to have been even greater in the many countries in which the troupes performed, and the often ornate language added to the difficulty for everyone.

Purposes of dialects

Luigi Riccobone, writing sometime between 1720 and 1730, thought that there was value in performing in different dialects, and amateur actor and theatre theorist

Andrea Perucci writing in 1699, assures us that the diversity of languages usually gives great pleasure in the comedy (cited in Clivio, 1989, p. 211; Perrucci, [1699] 2008, p. 130). Several contemporary scholars have tried to explain why this might be so. Gianrenzo Clivio supposes that part of the appeal of the dialects lay in their qualities of spontaneity, genuineness, and authenticity (Clivio, 1989, p. 215). The dialects were, as Flaminio Scala claimed commedia dell'arte in general was, imitative of nature (Scala, [1611] 1976, pp. cx–cxiii). Lower-class, and rural dialects, Clivio proposes, must have been a source of amusement for people who spoke, or thought they spoke, a more refined language (Clivio, 1989, p. 229). For instance, audience members could feel themselves superior to speakers of the rural version of the Bolognese dialect that the *zanni* played. The use of dialects, Marvin Carlson observes, tends to reinforce familiar comic stereotypes (Carlson, 2006, p. 77). Peter Burke comments that the actors' use of dialects inadvertently helped to disseminate their patron's agendas: "they mocked the very dialects they performed and they mocked idiolect and language blends, even while their communication depended on the audience's openness to it" (Burke, 2004, p. 80). And, finally, imperfect decoding on the part of the characters was a source of humor (Clivio, 1989, pp. 229–230).

Mitigating circumstances

Various writers have suggested mitigating factors in the difficulty of comprehension of the various dialects spoken by the actors. For the actors, themselves, there may not have been as much of a problem as we might suppose. According to Tommaso Garzoni (1585) actors had to be able to mimic every kind of speech. However, whether he meant that they could actually speak them is unclear because after specific examples of characters they could mimic, he extends his praise of their ability to mimic to all languages of the world (Garzoni cited in Marotti and Romei, 1991, p. 22). Mere mimicking may explain the mix of Spanish and an Italian dialect the captain spoke. Burke explains that turco was a mixture of Venetian with a Turkish accent and the odd Turkish word (2004, p. 135). Mimicking may have been a useful skill when, as frequently, characters disguised themselves as other characters like pilgrims and gypsies.

In her lifetime Isabella Andreini's verbal dexterity was admired. She seems to have spoken French. Whether she could also speak Spanish, Greek, and other languages, and all of the dialects spoken by the other characters, as an admirer from 1589 claimed, or whether she was able to effectively mimic multiple languages we do not know. Actor, *capocomico*, and theatre theorist Pier Maria Cecchini 1563-1645) was known have been able to speak Ferrarese, Florentine, Venetian, and Tuscan (Henke, 2002, p. 203). There were likely others who could speak in a variety of languages and dialects. Of necessity, actors may well have had at least a passive understanding of more languages and dialects than they spoke: troupes traveled to earn a living; their members would have to have understood something of local languages and dialects; they would also have to have been able to understand the other characters so that they could readily respond appropriately to them, even with deliberate misunderstandings.

There may have been mitigating circumstances for audience members as well. It seems likely that people in frontier areas between city-states in Italy and between Italy and nearby countries, including those with maritime connections, people at court, people in motion – like soldiers, merchants, pilgrims and refugees – or living in large urban areas where people from different parts of the country came together, particularly to engage in trade, or where they came from rural areas to find work in the city – would all have found communication with people outside their familiars imperative. Many people, then, seem likely to have gained at least a passive understanding of at least one language that they did not speak or spoke poorly.

It also seems likely that certain adjustments in the languages spoken were made for the various characters depending on where the troupe performed. Richard Andrews suggests that in Spanish garrison towns, the captain may have switched from Spanish to Neapolitan in order to be able to perform without censure in areas directly under Spanish control, principally, Naples, Sicily, Sardinia, and Milan (Andrews, 2008, p. xxxii).

Clivio (1989) believes that the *zanni* pushed their Bergamesque dialect in the direction of Venetian (p. 224). That would make sense because Richard Andrews describes the rural Bergamesque dialect as, even now in its modern form, incomprehensible to other Italians (2008, p. xxix). According to theatre commentator Andrea Perrucci ([1699] 2008), the Doctor's Bolgonese "need not be so rigorous in Naples, Palermo, or other cities far from Bologna, because it would not be understood; indeed it should be modified somewhat so that it is closer to Tuscan as spoken by the nobility of that illustrious city, not by the common people, whose language is scarcely intelligible" (p. 134). Clivio (1989) points to two tirades published by E. Petroccone that provide additional evidence that Graziano spoke a Tuscanized Bolognese (p. 220). And Clivio believes it likely that for the other dialects as well,

> certain adjustments must have been made more or less intuitively depending on the locality and the environment in which actors found themselves staging their plays, and the lexicon, at least, must have been tempered with lexemes of wide geographical distribution and, therefore, general intelligibility.
>
> (Clivio, 1989, p. 229)

All of this however was not enough to guarantee that full decodification existed (Clivio, 1989, pp. 210–211). Nonverbal elements must have played an important role.

Voice

Quintilian

Because voice is difficult to describe in words and because evidently no one thought to notate the speaking voice in commedia dell'arte, information about the sound of the voice in it is limited. The obvious place to turn, then, to try to learn about it is to information about instruction in oratorical delivery.

Oratory was an essential skill taught in the Renaissance in all the Latin grammar schools. Practically all sons of nobles and wealthy merchants and sons of professionals such as lawyers, physicians, notaries, high civil servants, university professors, and pre-university teachers would have attended such schools (Grendler, 1989, p. 102). Latin was the language of professional life, of administration, law, medicine, teaching, and the Church. It was the official language of instruction in all the universities and in Latin grammar schools across Europe. In these schools, speaking and writing were not regarded as separate skills. At the lowest levels of instruction, written declamations had to be spoken aloud from memory in class. And increasingly in the Renaissance attention was given to delivery – that is to voice and gesture (Mack, 2011, p. 313). It was understood that both could be taught.[5]

In the schools, Cicero was the most revered of classical orators and his speeches were extensively studied. But while delivery was for him one of the five essential parts of oratory, his *De oratore* (55 BCE 1977) has disappointingly little to say about that delivery. *Rhetorica ad Herennium*, formerly attributed to Cicero, and extremely influential in the Renaissance, specifies that rhetorical delivery includes voice quality and physical movement ([Cicero] [c. 80s, 90s BCE], 1954, p. 191), but it likewise tells us little about them. For a more expansive account of delivery, one has to turn to Quintilian's *Institutio oratoria* (95 CE, 2011), the aim of which was to educate the perfect orator. It was reprinted ninety-five times between 1470 and 1620. For many, it was the ultimate authority (Mack, 2011, p. 22.[6] Like Cicero, Quintilian was taught in schools of rhetoric throughout Latin speaking schools in western and central Europe (Sloane, 1997, 119). Book 11, Chapter 3 of Quintilian's twelve-volume work devotes some fifty pages to delivery, both voice and gesture.

Quintilian began first with voice: "We must first speak about voice, to which gesture also has to conform" (2001, p. 91).[7] According to him, it mattered less what was written than how it was uttered because "people are affected according to what they hear" (Quintilian, 2001, p. 87). Delivery in the theatre, Quintilian claimed, "has this power to produce anger, tears, or anxiety [even] over matters which we know to be fictitious and unreal" (p. 87). To be effective "the voice had to be varied, adapted to the nature of the subject of which we are speaking and of the feelings involved, so as not to be out of harmony with our words" (p. 107). At the same time, "if the Delivery is changed, the same words can "suggest, affirm, reproach, deny, wonder, show indignation, ask a question, mock, or disparage" (p. 177). Words are very powerful by themselves, but the voice adds its own contribution to the content, as do gestures and movements (p. 89).[8]

Quintilian's interest in evoking emotion must have met with a favorable response in the Renaissance when, according to Brian Vickers, during the second half of the sixteenth century and the first half of the seventeenth century, the role of the passions in persuasion became increasingly important. The resources of language became focused on the development of elocution in the service of persuasion.

Eloquent language served in all pursuits of public life; it was regarded as neither trivial nor decorative (Vickers, 1988, pp. 252–253). To be eloquent, according to Quintilian, language had to be ornate, that is, it had to have all the necessary inflections and tensions. One of the examples Quintilian provides is from Cicero's "splendid"– Quintilian's word – *Pro Milone*. It begins as follows: "Although I fear, members of the jury, that it is discreditable when beginning to speak on behalf of a very brave man, to feel afraid." This portion of the sentence, Quintilian explains is to begin in a restrained and subdued way and then become fuller and prouder when it comes to the topic of the very brave man. Then,

> the second breath has now to be stronger, both because of the natural effort which makes us speak the following words less timidly, and because Milo's courage is now to be shown: "and that it is very unbecoming when Titus Annius [Milo] is more troubled for the state's security than for his own." The new phrase is a sort of self-reproach: "that I should be unable to offer courage equal to his to serve his Cause."

After that, Quintilian explains, something more hard-hitting follows: " 'Nevertheless, the unprecedented court strikes terror into my eyes.' " And now the orator "opens practically every stop of his instrument: '. . . my eyes, which, wherever they fall, look in vain for the ordinary ways of the forum and the ancient procedures of our courts.' " What follows next vocally, Quintlian says, "is positively ample and diffuse: 'Your sitting is not, as it used to be, surrounded by a ring of spectators.' " Quintilian explains that he details all this "in order to make it clear that some variety of delivery should be provided not only in the longer units of the speech but also in the smaller ones" (pp. 105, 109, 111).

Visually, an extreme example of what Quintilian means by opening practically all the stops, as on an organ, comes from his instruction for the use of clothing in the course of an impassioned speech. The clothing is to become more and more disarrayed until finally, "when the great part of the speech is over . . . almost anything goes – sweat, fatigue, disordered clothing, toga loose and falling off all round. . . . I think that disheveled hair has some emotional impact, and wins approval just because trouble seems to have been forgotten" (pp. 161, 163). Elsewhere, he even considers tearing one's clothes as an appropriate gesture in pulling out all the stops (p. 177).

The voice should be higher when the emotions are high and dropped when they are calmer. For example, "the highest – most penetrating tone available to an orator should be heard in 'When the war was begun, Caesar, indeed when it was almost done.' " Then with " 'What was that sword of yours doing, Tubero, on the field of Pharsalus,' " it should be slightly lower and with a touch of charm. This is to be followed by a delivery "fuller, slower, and so easier on the ear," with the words "drawn out, the vowels lengthened, and the throat opened" on " 'in an assembly of the Roman people, performing his official functions.' " Then "the stream flows fuller still in: 'Ye hills and groves of Alba' until finally there is "something of a chanting effect in the gradual fall of 'Rocks and deserts responds to the voice' " (p. 173).

Quintilian goes on to provide examples where one might use extraordinary harshness, almost beyond the scope of the human voice, a tearful sweetness, and, in lamenting, a kind of singing tone. In the epilogue to *Pro Milone*, he says, the confession of being overcome by grief and fatigue expressed in the words, " 'I can no longer speak for tears' " is to be delivered in a manner corresponding to the words. And there should be passages which have "infinitely more inflection and modulation: 'O miserable, unhappy me!' 'What shall I reply to my children?' " (pp. 175).

In his concluding section on delivery Quintilian states that different speakers have identifiably different ways of speaking. Finally, he reminds the would-be orator, as did Cicero, that moderation rules both in voice and gesture: "I do not want my pupil to be a comic actor, but an orator" (p. 181). Given his explanation about how one might dramatically use one's clothing to advantage, it is hard to know what this means for the orator – or for the comic actor. We know that voice and gesture are to conform to one another.

We obviously have to ask to what extent theatre audiences and actors, for that matter, were familiar with Quintilian's instruction. Some of the actors were well-educated and evidently schooled in Latin grammar schools. Further, commedia actors, in addition to improvised performances, performed written comedy. It seems highly likely that initially performances of the written comedy, the *commedia erudite*, modeled on classical texts and performed by gentlemen in their learned societies, used the means of delivery learned in their education in oratory in the Latin grammar schools and in the universities.[9] The relationship between oratory and acting was explicit: at least in the Jesuit schools "the association of acting with the teaching of rhetoric in humanist schools is a well-known fact" (Murphy, 1983, p. 102). To what extent the professional actors used these same means of delivery as well as the texts of the learned comedy cannot be known.

The populace in general would have been regularly present at Church sermons and its Mass. Peter Burke calls attention to the work of Gian Luigi Beccaria who claims that even today the various dialects are full of liturgical Latin, however well or ill understood or used in mockery (Burke, 2004, p. 50). Along with the Latin, the congregants would likely have become familiar with the way in which it was spoken.

The general populace would also have been present at public orations and, on occasion, at legal proceedings. Centuries before, Cicero had turned the orator into a cultural hero (Vickers, 1988, p. 172). And that respect for the orator continued in the Renaissance. There was evidently considerable interest in public speaking even among the general populace.

Wilbourne

In her book on the origins of opera, Emily Wilbourne (2016) focuses on the aural dimension of commedia dell'arte performance to explain the inspiration for and ready acceptance of early Italian opera. "The [supposed] leap from spoken to sung drama is largely negated by an acknowledgment that the spoken theater relied in large part on the communicative and signifying capacities of sound itself" (Wilbourne, 2016, p. 153).[10] In commedia dell'arte there was, Wilbourne argues, a marked distance between regular speech and dramatic declamation. That declamation prepared audiences to accept the music of opera because its sound was already familiar; early opera simply took the established vocal conventions of dramatic speech. Just as commedia's imitation of an action was not the action itself, but something exaggerated, heightened, and codified into a standard set of tropes, so too were the sonic elements of its linguistic communication (p. 155). These are bold ideas.

Key to Wilbourne's argument is a single paragraph she came across written by the musician and composer Vincenzo Galilei in 1581. The paragraph makes his recommended relationship between commedia dell'arte and early music explicit in some detail and Wilbourne makes inspired use of it throughout her work. Galilei (the father of Galileo), Wilbourne tells us, was a seminal figure in the musical life of the late Renaissance and contributed significantly to the musical revolution that demarcates the beginning of the Baroque era. So his advice probably carried weight. Galilei counseled composers to restrain their immoderate laughter when attending performances of the commedia dell'arte and listen instead to its sounds because from these they could take the musical expression of any idea that came to mind (Wilbourne, p. 1). Galilei details the rich expressiveness of the speaking voice in commedia dell'arte replete, he says, with changes in "pitch (high or low), volume of sound, accents and gestures, speed [and] slowness of articulation."

Each kind of character – married woman, girl, or clever harlot – according to Galilei, had a distinct identifiable sound. Distinctive vocal identities were associated with each role and each individual character had an identifiable vocal signature (Wilbourne, p. 156). Further, according to Galilei, there was a clear aural distinction between various interactions, for instance between when two gentlemen speak quietly together and when one of them speaks to a servant (p. 1). Early modern audiences could not only take pleasure in these variations in sounds in themselves, Wilbourne deduces, but also, from them, they could obtain many contextual cues and much narrative content (p. 26). Voices differed relative to nationality, regionality, age, health, sex, education, social status, occupation and sincerity (p. 152). "The polyphony of the dialect in commedia dell'arte served as a singularly effective medium with which to transmit characterological information, and the experience of the dell'arte theatre relied on a musicalization of listening in order to make dramatic sense" (pp. 48–49).

The aural dimension according to Galilei also makes clear distinctions between emotional states, between, for instance how someone laments, and how someone exults in joy. Female lovers would have responded in consistent, recognizable sonic figurations for each emotion and situation. Ordinarily women, Wilbourne claims,

> declaimed their lines in a noble, restrained fashion; the ardent lover, on the other hand, must have found a sonic means to express her giddy state of being in love, either by quite literally breaking into the ebullient rhythms of florid

> song or by an explosive, energetic diction that would have communicated the same affect.
>
> (p. 159)

While educated listeners might have understood references to literary works in the monologs of the *innamorata*, others with less education, Wilbourne observes, would have heard only the florid language and elevated metric structure. In that case, particularly, the spoken theatre relied in large part on the communicating and signifying capacity of sound itself (pp. 49–50).

Dialects, strong identifiers of character, had distinctly different sounds, even though some shared mostly similar vocabularies. Audience members' understanding varied depending on the region in which they lived and the nature of their daily interactions in the cosmopolitan aspects of the area in which they lived (p. 153). In all cases the listeners' understanding was only partial.

Instead of wrestling with the difficulties this partial comprehension presented, and explaining the ways in which they may have been ameliorated, as have theatre historians, Wilbourne, a musicologist, is not at all bothered by the difficulties: "commedia dell'arte theater succeeded not in spite of its moments of unintelligibility, but because the sound of the words remained meaningful even where the words themselves were impossible to understand" (p. 50). The audience members of the commedia dell'arte could interpret theatrical aurality. Unconsciously they decoded [and again she cites Galilei], "'pitch (high or low), volume of sound, accents and gestures, speed [and] slowness of articulation' in order to make sense of the sound" (p. 50).

The relative incomprehensibility of commedia performance served as a source of humor and signification beyond words (p. 50). Thus, comments Wilbourne, when Graziano mixed Latin with Bolgonese, it was not important that his audience understood every word of his speech; in fact Graziano's ability to transcend the comprehension of the audience with his pseudo-intellectual talk was an integral part of his verbal "schtick." The sound of his speech conveyed as much or more than his words. His Bolognese called up a university town; the audience could hear his pomposity, his self-importance, and his desire to lecture (p. 23).

To support Galilei's recommendation that the voice in opera ought to follow that in commedia, Wilbourne provides examples from early operas and their librettos, of performers who moved fluidly between acting and singing roles, and of play texts written by Giovanni Battista Andreini, son of the famous commedia dell'arte actors Francesco and Isabella Andrerini, from which the relationship between commedia and early opera can be inferred.

Wilbourne's reading of Galilei also directs her attention to the words written on voice by two men of the theatre: Pier Maria Cecchini ([1608] 1991) and amateur actor Andrea Perrucci ([1699] 2008). Their descriptions of vocal variations, she suggests, ought no longer to be passed over casually. Cecchini tells us that "just as the words are varied, so variously one lets them out" (cited in Wilbourne, 2016, p. 157). And Perrucci, after he presents a long list of vocal variations, concludes that the voice, "should be varied, as was said earlier, according to circumstances, seeking to move the spectators' emotions by using different sounds" (Wilbourne, 2016, p. 157).[11]

Definite confirmation of Galilei's statement about the distance of the voice from ordinary speech in commedia dell'arte is provided by *Il corago*, an anonymous treatise written by a composer sometime between 1628 and 1637, some fifty years after Galilei's fruitful paragraph. "Perfection" of recitative – *Il corago* limits himself to recitative – is achieved 'through the variety and imitation of the melodic invention . . . used by those who are esteemed by all the best actors and most affecting public speakers" (Wilbourne, 2016, p. 70). It would even be helpful, *Il corago* says, "to hear those same verses that one has to set to music recited first by a worthy and expressive actor because . . . recitative is nothing other than a modulated imitation of a perfect recitation" (pp. 154–155).[12]

Gesture according to the *Il corago*, citing Quintilian, is "*pronuntiatio corporis*" (bodily enunciation) (p. 158). Wilbourne believes that when *Il corago* states that "in the act of rage, gestures should be fierce and aggressive, moving the hand with more or less fury according to the words," we should assume that the movements of the voice are comparable to the gestures (p. 158). There are alterations of the voice according to the diversity of things narrated, just as there are gestures to suit the words. Voice and gesture are inextricably linked and they should be consistent with the phrases of the wording (p. 158).

Both Galilei and *Il Corago*, Wilbourne sums up, "turned to a preexisting theatrical idiom in which the sonic and gestural elements of linguistic communication were already exaggerated, heightened, and codified into a set of standard tropes" (Wilbourne, 2016, p. 155). For me, the sonic element in that "preexisting theatrical idiom" evokes Quintilian, who asks "does not even Cicero say that there is a sort of muffled song in oratory?" (Quintilian, 2001, pp. 114–115).

Gesture

For people who study language and cognition, gesture is "all bodily action that is considered to be a part of a person's willful expression" (Kendon, 2000, p. ix). Gesture was undoubtedly an aid to verbal comprehension in Renaissance Italy. According to contemporary commentators from outside Italy, Italians, more than any other Europeans, engaged in the language of gesture. Herman Roodenburg cites a Dutchman, who, in 1735, concluded that the Italians, who "speak with their head, arms, feet and the whole body" are simply the antithesis of all civility (Roodenburg, 1992, p. 160). It was likely that this perceived lack of civility serves in part to account for the widespread success of commedia dell'arte performance.

The extensive and specific use of gesture helped the performers in a bustling noisy piazza attract attention and communicate with their audience. Gesture helped to communicate across the many Italian dialects, and in many European countries. It also served in the commedia to provide silent asides and side interchanges surreptitiously conducted with a third party, and for lovers to communicate silently between the balcony and the street. The gestural differences between young and old, male and female, respectable and shameless, noble and common, Spanish and Italian, etc. served as ready guides to character identification (Burke, 1992, p. 75). We can reasonably infer that gesture among lower-class characters was broad because of the many treatises intended for members of the nobility, the well-to-do, and the clergy recommending restraint in gesture (Burke, 1992, p. 76). An upper-class woman, like the *innamorata*, would have been instructed to observe *modestia*, to avoid pomp and ostentation in her gestures and deportment, to hold her head still in order to keep her eyes from wandering, and to speak seldom (Knox, 2000, p. 6).[13] The Spanish, on the other hand, including the Spanish captains of the scenarios, were perceived as haughty swaggerers, full of mock gallantry and euphuisms (Boughner, 1954, p. 76). Audience members came to learn the range of each individual character's behavior and emotions and the nature of their interactions with other people and from these to a certain extent they could reasonably guess what was being said.[14] Pantalone was given to rage against his children and his servants and to inappropriate infatuations with young women. *Lazzi* (gags) engaged in by the *zanni* were primarily visual. Beyond that, it is useful to look at what visual and verbal information we have about gesture from the period.

Pictorial aids

The meaning of many gestures in the visual arts of Renaissance Italy can be readily understood outside Italy now four hundred years after the golden age of commedia dell'arte. Thus Stefan Hulfeld (2014) aided by the scenarios' texts, unhesitatingly describes the actions in each of the watercolors serving as frontispieces to the Corsini scenarios, often including descriptions of the use of the hands, and the pictures provide no reason to challenge his interpretations (Figure 2.1, p. 36).

Even without reference to the scenarios one can readily identify many of the gestures in the watercolors: threatening, pleading, crying, praying, pointing, or otherwise calling attention to something, welcoming, showing astonishment, lolling about, showing maidenly modesty, and embracing in love. Similarly, in viewing M.A. Katritzky's (2006) ambitious collection of pictures contemporary with and referencing commedia dell'arte performance, one can recognize the meaning of these same gestures as well as those of horror, dismay, toasting, asking someone to "wait-up," listening, imploring, being upset by a duel, amazement, making sexual advances, and more.[15] Moshe Barasch (1976) amply shows us gestures of despair in Italian Renaissance painting: breast-beating, hair tearing, and hand-biting.

Visual images, however, do not show the movement of gestures, and many frequently used gestures, like nodding the head to indicate assent, are totally dependent upon movement. Nor do visual images show the pace of the individual gestures, or the frequency of gestures, their sequencing, or their correlation with verbal phrasing, and there is a limit to the information they can convey about spoken words. If we turn to written works, we find that these too have their limitations.

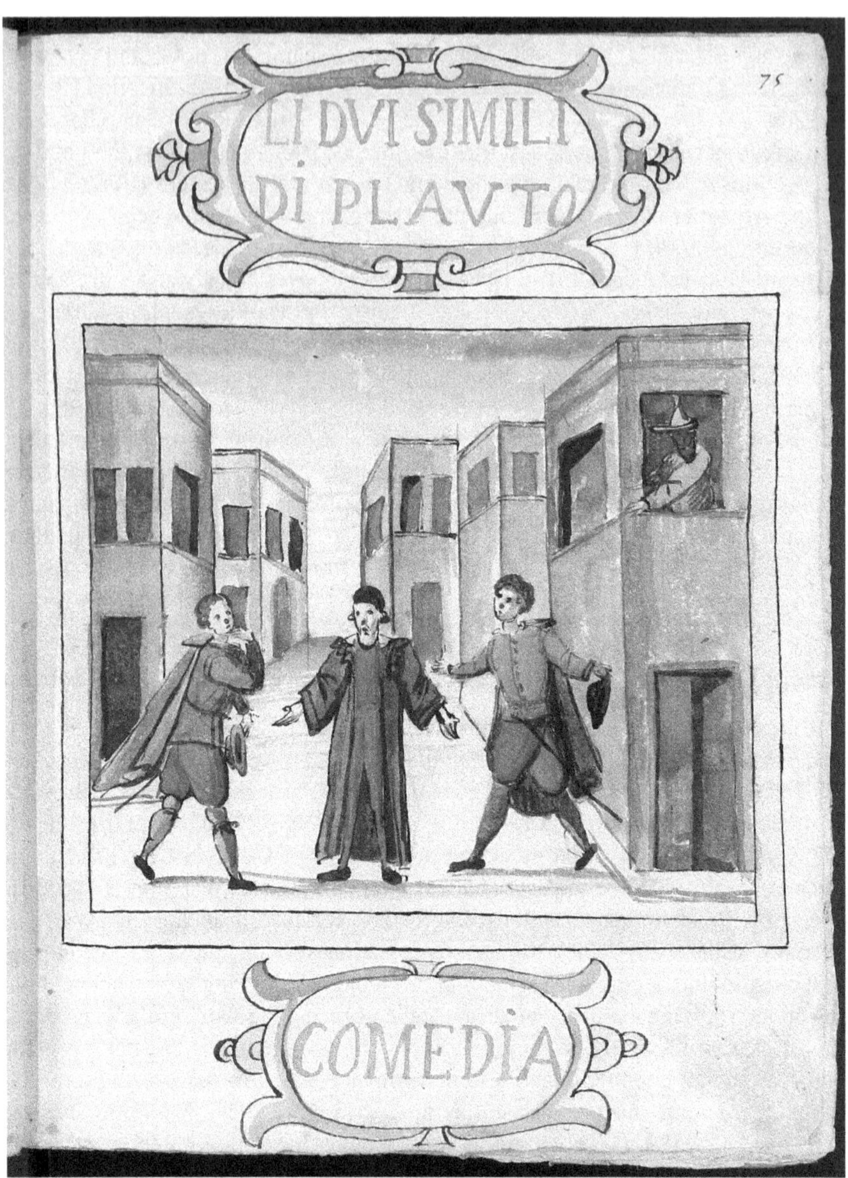

Figure 2.1 "The illustration shows the meeting of two twins, Capitanio and Silvio, after many confusions. While one twin approaches the other with open arms, the other holds his hand in a hesitant or surprised way. Pantalone stands bewildered between them, while Zanni at the window is astonished at what has happened" (Hulfeld, p. 351, my translation). Whether the gesture of the Zanni, which, in effect, serves to call attention to the meeting of the brothers is a pictorial convention or whether on the stage his gesture might also deliberately serve to call attention to the action is unknown.

Source: Frontispiece "*Li dui simili di Plauto.*" (n.d.). Anonymous pen and watercolor. "*Raccolta di scenari più scelti d'istrioni divisi in due volume.*" (Biblioteca Corsiniana, Rome). MS 45.G. 5. Vol. 1, number 11. By permission of the Accademia Nazionale dei Lincei e Corsiniana.

Written aids

Shakespeare

Two fine books have examined Shakespeare's descriptions of gestures in detail (Bevington, 1984; Karim-Cooper, 2016). Bevington notes that "conventional gestural language of Shakespeare's age "owed its visually predictable character to the assumption that gesture and emotions were generated by fixed physiological processes" (1984, p. 68). Dramatists found a way of suiting action to emotion in ways that would have been understood throughout Europe. These ways were disseminated in popular lore and in both dramatic and non-dramatic literature (Bevington, 1984, p. 70). They arose from the medical doctrine of the humors, widely accepted throughout Europe. Bevington gives an example of anger as a manifestation of the humors: anger is something very physical, described by one writer in 1625 as "a shaking of the hands and lips, paleness, or redness, or swelling of the face, glaring of the eyes, stammering of the tongue, stamping with the feet, unsteady motions of the whole body, rash actions, which we remember not to have done, distracted and wild speeches" (Bevington, 1984, p. 69).

Although Shakespeare also used more nuanced gestures, an authentic performance of his work in 1600, would strike us nonetheless as "quaintly formal to the extent that its acting conventions would reflect a hierarchical society and a symbolic mode of thought very distant from our own." Further, the outdoor stage required that the gestures would have to have been large and the delivery bold (Bevington, 1984, p. 71). These and other observations would seem readily applicable to commedia dell'arte in the period under examination.

One must be cautious however in relying on Shakespeare to determine particular gestures used in commedia dell'arte. Desmond Morris, et al., in their study of the distribution of gestures in Europe in use in 1979, the date of their book, made clear that the recognition and meaning of the distinctive gestures they selected, "the teeth flick," "the ear touch," "the nose tap," for instance, varied widely in distribution. Some, like thumbing one's nose in mockery, were widespread, others were not, or took on different meaning in different places. For instance, making the hand into a purse was recognized throughout Italy as making a query; in France, it was taken to express fear.

Bonifaccio and de Jorio

One assumes that books on gesture from Italy might be a safer source. In Venice in 1616, Giovanni Bonifaccio published his *L'arte de'cenni*, a 624-page book, intended as a comprehensive survey of all the signs that he thought possible to make with bodily action and with clothing and ornamentation.[16] His hope in writing the book was to show that gesture was the most expressive and universal language and that it could serve to replace the existing Tower of Babel of spoken languages.

Alas, Bonifaccio bolsters his argument by bringing in the most authoritative sources he could think of: the Bible, and classical, medieval, and Renaissance sources. And while the continuity of some gestures can be traced back to the classical period – bowing your head as a sign of reverence, for instance (Bonifaccio, 1616, p. 19), in general, we cannot say which or how many of the gestures Bonifaccio presents were in use in Renaissance Italy or that they were in use in all of Italy. Interestingly, Morris et al. were able to trace the 1979 use of the head toss to signify negation in the area around Naples directly back to Naples' ancient colonization by the Greeks, who continue to use the head toss, precisely because the gesture was not recognized elsewhere in Italy (Morris et al., 1979, pp. 247–259). We do not know what the effect of Bonifaccio's effort might have been. His book went through only one printing. Dilwyn Knox finds no evidence that the book was influential (1991, p. 396, note 40).

I depart briefly from the seventeenth century to consider a book from 1832 because its author, Andrea de Jorio, believed that through careful documentation of street gesture in Naples at the time, he could read the gestures found in classical mosaic, frescoes, vases and statues, particularly those unearthed in Herculaneum and Pompeii, both near Naples (de Jorio, [1832] 2000; Kendon, 2000). If this were so, logically, such a continuum of gesture in time ought to allow us to know the nature of gesture in Italy in the seventeenth century. Unlike Bonifaccio whose compendium begins with the head and moves down through the feet, de Jorio organizes the gestures alphabetically. His book continues to be regarded as a fine record of gesture in 1832 Naples, but, according to Kendon, who has written an invaluable history of the study of gesture, the book is unfortunately not now widely accepted as a resource for the interpretation of ancient artwork (Kendon, 2004, p. 45). I do note that, beginning with de Jorio's first gesture "*abbracciare*" (embrace), an embrace is still an embrace; pregnancy or corpulence can still be indicated by bringing the arms down in a large circle in the area of one's belly, and one can still call attention to something ("*additare*") with a feigned cough, with the thumb extended and directed to the object, or, even more discretely, with eyes and head turned briefly in the direction of that to which one wishes to call attention. These gestures have continued to be meaningful well beyond Naples for a period of almost two hundred years. But other gestures are not familiar. It is hard to say with any assurance what de Jorio might have to tell us about gesture in early-seventeenth-century Italy beyond Naples.

Caroso

A trustworthy, although limited, book for learning about gesture for the period 1570–1630 is Fabritio Caroso's *Nobiltà di dame* ([1600] 1995). This is one of a number of books on dance written in Italy at the time: Cesare Negri's *Le gratie d'omore*, 1602 and 1604, which includes music, and the more limited works without music, by Livio Lupi (1600, 1607) and Prospero Lutius (1587, 1589), and Caroso's own *Il ballarino*, 1581, an earlier version of *Nobiltà di dame* but with more dances and their music. But *Nobiltà di dame* corrects and further clarifies instructions for the dances and correlates the music with them. It also includes pictures of couples in their beginning positions for the various dances. Of particular interest relative to consideration of gesture is its inclusion of sixteen pages on the "Conduct Required of Gentlemen and Ladies at a Ball and Elsewhere" (Sutton, 1995).[17] Italy dominated Europe in the realm of social dance for balls and weddings among the aristocracy. Its various dancing masters taught, not only in Italy, but also in Spain, France, the Netherlands, and the German-speaking countries. Italian dances are present in Shakespeare's plays (Sutton, 1995, p. 24). So we can be pretty sure that that the influence of Italian teaching about proper behavior for upper-class social dance, as well as more generally, reached throughout the continent and into England as well.[18]

Caroso's information on proper etiquette includes advice on how a gentleman should wear his cape and on how the cape should be arranged so that the sword, which he wears so that he can be at the ready even while dancing (in order to protect the lady [Sutton, 1991]), how and when to remove one's gloves, kiss one's hand and extend it to a partner, enact reverence, sit (for ladies how to sit without the hoop skirt revealing their knees or beyond), doff one's hat, and more. Sutton tells us that doffing one's hat was appropriate before God, one's master, and a lady (Sutton, 1991). Erect posture, quiet arms, a level gaze and straight legs are important for ladies and gentlemen and not just while dancing (Sutton, 1995, pp. 26, 368). So some of the etiquette described was useful not only for actors playing upper-class characters but also for those playing the captain or servants. Warnings about what not to do call to mind the behavior of Captain Spavento:

> unnecessary, empty and precious courtesies are scarce-hidden flatteries; too many Reverences (by sliding their feet, kissing their hands or doffing their bonnets while bowing and scraping before their favourite ladies) lose just as much [favour in the eyes of others][19] as they think to gain, for their blandishments only displease and bore them. Others are too verbose and overly polite in order to compensate for the defects of their base and lowly natures.
>
> (Sutton, 1995, pp. 139–140)

Quintilian

The broader range of descriptions of gesture in Shakespeare, and in books by Bonifaccio and de Jorio, importantly include gestures to express emotions, as the books on dancing certainly do not, but, as I have said, they leave open questions about the distribution of these gestures in time and over space. It may seem surprising, given my concern about the continuity of gesture over time and space, that the teachings I think most instructive about gesture in commedia dell'arte is Quintilian's *Instituto oratoria* (95 CE). But its first value is its widespread use in Renaissance education throughout Europe.

While Cicero (*De oratore* (1977, p. 179) tells us that "by action the body talks, his remarks on gesture are regretably even more limited than those on voice. Quintilinan, however, describes not only specific gestures that should be used by orators and those that should not be used because they are lower class or too theatrical, but also how frequent gestures should be and where they should be placed in a speech.

It is not clear how many of Quintilian's gestures would have to have been learned in the Renaissance and how many would have been familiar because they were still in common use. It seems likely that those in attendance at a Church service would have come to recognize the gestures used, themselves directly influenced by the teaching of gesture in the Latin grammar schools. For the unschooled, some catechisms taught doctrine and morals with the aid of picture books replete with gestures "for the simple and those who do not know how to read" (Grendler, 1989, p. 354). The gestures in them would have been drawn by those trained in the Latin grammar schools. Many gestures in Quintilain would be understood and might well be used today: "when we have to say something which is particularly impressive and rich . . . the arm sweeps out to the side and the language somehow expands with the Gesture"; "the hand may also be drawn towards the body, with the fingers pointing down a little more freely, and then opening more widely to face the opposite way, so that it seems to be somehow delivering our actual words"; "a gesture particularly well adapted to an expression of modesty consists in bringing the thumb and the first three fingers gently together to a point, and moving the hand towards the body in the region of the mouth or chest, then letting it fall, palm downwards and slightly brought forward" (Quintilian, 2001, pp. 121, 129, 135). Gestures in Quintilian for indicating modesty and the restraint indicating timidity would suit the *innamorata*: "The Hand slightly curved (as though expressing support), and moved short distances to the accompaniment of a small shoulder movement, is a Gesture which is particularly appropriate for the restrained speaker who wishes to give an impression of timidity" (p. 137). The watercolor of Corsini 1/43, "La pazzia di Doralice" (Figure 2.2, p. 41) makes clear that Doralice is mad because her flailing arms above and beyond all bounds of modesty and her hair in disarray show that she has abandoned all lady-like decorum.

The most important guidance Quintilian provides about gesture, however, sets his work apart from that I have previously discussed because it lays out general guidelines about the interrelationship between words, gesture, and voice, and between gestures. As Darren Tunstall observed "the total meaning of a segment of movement involves *clusters* of behavior in a given context" (2016, p. 19). Gesture is to conform to the voice (Quintilian, 2001, p. 119). It should follow the breath and begin or end with the sense (p. 141). But also gesture should be used sometimes for marking pauses even within sentences and without a new breath. The sentence beginning "'*in coetu vero populi Romani, negotium publicum gerens, magister equitum*, and so on, [Truly, in the assembly of the Roman people, bearing on the public business, a member of the equestrian order] has many Cola (there are a number of thoughts, one after another but only one Period; so it is a case for short pauses between these phrases, not for breaking up the structure of the whole" (pp. 103, 105). Gesture should be consistent with the units of speech (p. 141). So in this case, it would seem that each phrase is to be marked by a separate gesture: four gestures in ten words. While the hand should not be in continuous motion fragmenting the delivery by continual movement, it should not rest idle for long (p. 141).

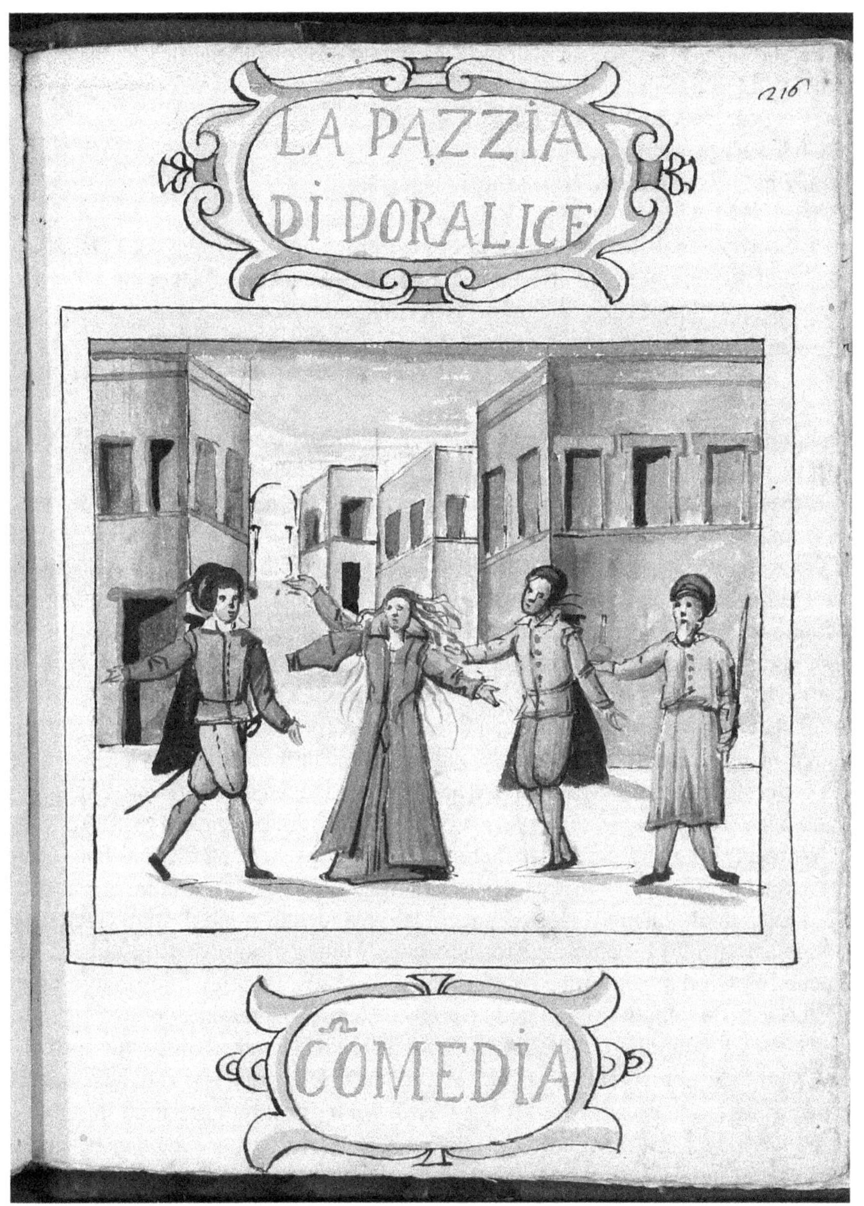

Figure 2.2 Frontispiece "*La pazzia di Doralice.*" (n.d.). Anonymous pen and watercolor. "*Raccolta di scenari più scelti d'istrioni divisi in due volume.*"

Source: Accademia Nazionale dei Lincei e Corsiniana.

Gestures are to be made primarily with the right hand, although the left hand can add emphasis (p. 143).[20] It is best for the hand to begin its movement on the left and end it on the right (p. 139). The use of the two hands together produces more emotion. When the subject is unimportant, unthreatening or sad, hands are to be held close to the body; with grander themes, or when joy or outrage is called for, they can be thrust further forward (p. 145).

On the stage, according to Quintilian, phrasing and their gestures is no different from what it is in oratory. When the actor says,

> "So what shall I do? Not go, not even now when I am sent for? Or rather, steel myself not to put up with insults from these harlots?" Here the actor will introduce pauses for hesitation, inflections of voice, various hand-gestures, and different movements of the hand.
>
> (pp. 181, 183)

That would seem to amount to four or five gestures. When the passion goes up, gesture too will become more frequent (p. 243).

Movement in comedy is faster than in tragedy. The movement of young men, old men, soldiers, and married women advances sedately; that of the lower class is faster (p. 143). Quintilian's warnings about what orators ought not to do might well guide actors performing commedia dell'arte's comic lower-class characters: holding the feet too far apart is unsightly if you are standing still and almost indecent combined with movement (p. 152). Shrugged or hunched shoulders shorten the neck suggesting humiliation, servility, and hypocrisy because people use it when they are pretending to flatter, admire, or fear (pp. 127–129). They seem well-suited to the *zanni* (comic servants or, less frequently, other lower-class comic characters). Putting the right foot and hand forward together is a gesture belonging to comedy rather than of oratory (p. 149). So is the trembling hand (p. 139).

Without citing any particular rhetorician, but consistent with Quintilian, Matthew Buckley (2009, p 253) has argued for commedia's "appropriation of classical vocabularies of manual rhetoric," specifically handedness and posture (including stance and stride) by attending to their use in the well-known woodcuts in the Recueil Fossard album probably from the mid 1580s. Buckley finds that in them gestures made with the right hand "carried a clear connotation of power, agency, potency and rectitude, "whereas gestures with the left hand signified "loss, weakness, inefficacy, impotence or error." Pantalone's right hand, Buckley observes, is never quite at the proper level. It is either down by his groin or raised in outrage or command (p. 259). An upright stance with feet close to one another bespeaks high status and moral integrity but a lowered pose, wide stance, and bowed back convey scheming, weakness, impropriety, and servitude (260).[21]

Flaminio Scala[22]

At the last, I focus on Flaminio Scala's invaluable collection of scenarios and the extent to which it allows us to make deductions about the acting style, particularly about gesture. By the time of Scala's collection of fifty scenarios, *Il teatro delle favole rappresentative*, Scala was a well-established actor/manager of the commedia dell arte. Scala wrote that for his publication he had collected together scenarios that he had originally composed for occasional performance on public stages, at which time he had no thought of publishing them (Scala, [1611] 1976, p.2). When he did decide to publish them, he probably provided more detail than he would have provided for professional performers because, he said, he also intended them for readers. Nonetheless, recent scholarship has come to accept them as reliable guides to professional performance (Fitzpatrick, 1995, *passim*; Henke, 2002, p. 13; Galli, 2005, p. 122 and *passim*).

Indeed, because of their enhancement, they serve as the best scenarios to examine for information about the style of commedia dell'arte performance. They only rarely provide us with dialogue but rather with such a wealth of descriptions of emotions, motivations, and actions that it is, in fact, possible to reconstruct performance from them with some degree of reliability.[23] Other collections of the period, like the Corsini and Locatelli collections, often rely on a kind of shorthand strictly for actors, for instance, "They have their scene," "He replies with his trick of 'Didn't I tell you I didn't believe it?,'" and "They have their by-play" are considerably less helpful for readers today (Lea, [1934] 1962, *passim pp. 555–674).*

Typical passages from Scala's Act II of Day 27, *La mancata fede*, for instance, provide some idea of the wealth of descriptions of actions and emotions in the scenarios. The following selected passages from that act are sequential but they do not allow readers to make out anything of the plot. Rather, I have selected them to call attention to the evidence of acting style:

> He [Burattino] . . . makes passes at her and tries to kiss her, and she [Flaminia dressed as a pilgrim] scolds him. . . . Flavio [enters] grieving over what Pantalone has told him. . . . He falls into despair. . . . Orazio comes from his house, all sad and melancholy. . . . Orazio bursts into tears. [Isabella in disguise as male] starts weeping "himself". Orazio complains. . . . Pedrolino enters and recognizes Isabella; next Flavio enters and also recognizes her, but is doubtful. Isabella, seeing him, immediately covers her face with her cloak and exits, so as not to be recognized. . . . Flaminia who has been at the door and recognized her father Pedrolino, and also recognized Isabella, takes Orazio by the hand and leads him indoors. Burattino [who believes Isabella to be a beardless youth] is amazed at this action.
>
> (Andrews, 2008, pp. 154–155)

Burattino and Pedrolino, the servants in these passages were probably masked, although Pedrolino may have been performed in white face. The other characters, the lovers, were probably not masked.[24] The character masks for the comic characters, including those of the servants, were partial: half or three-quarters, and permitted the mouth and eyes to be seen. Thus, they allowed a significant amount of facial expressivity. The masks themselves, with the head turned this way and that, upward or downward and front, side, or three-fourths could also be quite expressive. But the actions and emotions described are such that the face with or without a mask did not suffice to express them.

In addition to the use of the body for the expression of meanings and emotions, Scala specified that various of the characters required other physical skills: the ability to engage in sword play, to dance, sing, and play musical instruments. The role of Arlecchino required that he be able to carry other actors and perform stunts with traveling bags and trunks and, in two scenarios, with a ladder.

The emotions described in the scenarios are characteristically very strong: weeping, rage, love, fear, amazement madness, grief, and jealousy. David Bevington has remarked regarding performances of Shakespeare in the period that "strong passions call for vivid acting, and Shakespeare wrote for spectators who were familiar with a lore of conventional signs through which Renaissance students of behavior cataloged the predicable physical manifestations of potent inner distress" (Bevington, 1984, p. 81). Just how strong the emotions were and how vivid the acting to represent them was necessitated for performing the Scala scenarios is perhaps made clearest by the frequency with which anger among young men leads to duels, by the number of instances in which characters, both male and female, faint from shock, or engage in weeping in scenes of extended and contagious weeping that would have necessitated something considerably more exaggerated than tears.

The response to Isabella's disguise in the passages from *La mancata fede* provided allows us to make further inferences about the style of the acting than that it was very physical. When Pedrolino recognizes Isabella, he would have to have done so through gesture or by means of an aside, or both. Similarly, Flavio. But Flavio, by the same means, had also to express doubt about his identification of the supposed youth as Isabella. Burattino never sees through Isabella's disguise at all. This means that Isabella's costume disguise and acting as a youth had to have been such that at the same time they could be seen through, including by the audience, and yet persuasively convincing to Burattino.

Scala specifies that Isabella, in disguise as a youth, wears a cape – like that a gentleman would wear. She was also likely to have been wearing breeches, a hat, and a sword. She probably also attempted a male walk and gestures and employed speech in a lower register. Laura Giannetti Ruggiero points to the ease with which girls could have passed as youths in the society because of the late onset of puberty and because of the perceived androgyny of adolescents (Giannetti Ruggiero, 2005, pp. 743–760). On the other hand, the perceived androgyny could never have been altogether absolute in the drama, because for the humor to have been effective, the audience had to have known that the male or female disguise was only that. The disguise would have to have made its deployment comic and call attention to the art of acting but if it was too obviously a disguise, the audience could not successfully have accepted the idea that characters were fooled by it, nor could they have had the pleasure of seeing an actor play two quite different roles well. The many disguise roles in the scenarios, most of them convincing to the other characters, suggest that this pleasure of one character impersonating another with some degree of success, was an important one for the audience. It would have required acting skill.

The disguise not only called attention to the character disguised, it also called attention to the actor performing the character affecting the disguise. The clearest example of this is when, to escape an unacceptable situation, a female character played mad. Madness was primarily represented through speech and song.[25] But, as in the Corsini watercolor serving as preface for the scenario 1/43, "La pazzia da Doralice," (Figure 2.2, p. 41) typically madness was, also, in part, represented by hair and clothing in disarray, rent, or even partially removed. In Canto 23 of Ludovico Ariosto's extremely influential epic poem, *Orlando furioso*, 1532, Orlando, become mad, "worked into a great frenzy . . . he tore off his clothes."[26] Traditionally, those who reduced their apparel to rags or cast away body coverings repudiated their place in the social hierarchy (Valesio, 1971 p. 203; Salkeld, 1993, p. 109).[27] It was assumed that no sane person of status would do that. Madness could be real, as well as a disguise. Mad, the character was known on occasion to tear her clothes asunder and bare her breasts not only because madness was viewed as a descent into a lower state of being, but also because the breast-baring was a crowd-pleaser excused by the pretend or actual madness of the character. Of course, in the process, not only was the breast of the character exposed but also that of the actress. The distinction between actor and role was thus radically elided. The seemingly all-out rage, jealousy, fear, grief, and love, characteristic of the Scala scenarios, particularly in the culture that increasingly valued affect control (Biow, 2010, p. 182), must often have resulted in an apparent or actual synthesis of character and actor, as did the ostensibly improvised performance itself. Both made the relationship of actor and audience quite intimate.

The female character and actress disguised as male in *La mancata fede* and in many other scenarios, necessarily called attention to the fact that gender roles were assumed, not essential. In fact, the many disguise roles, more largely reflected a society in which the public self was a construct. Everyday life required the careful management of impressions. The *sprezzatura* Baldesar Castiglione recommended for courtiers, the cool nonchalance that concealed all art and made whatever they said or did appear to be effortless and almost without any thought about it, was a kind of disguise (Castiglione, [1967] 1976, pp. xxvi–xxviii). The culture of craft and craftiness was omnipresent. The Venetian lawyer and historian Paolo Sarpi observed in 1609, that he was, in effect, "obliged to wear a mask, because no one in Italy may go without one" (cited in Snyder, 2009, p. 59). The mask was a common metaphor for dissimulation in early modern culture. No one knew with certainty whether the face was "already a mask and its owner no different than an actor in a comedy: in the culture of secrecy, the natural was always already artificial" (cited in Snyder, 2009, p. 6). Imposters were potentially everywhere. It was an age of dissimulation in Europe (Snyder, 2009 pp. 5, 59). The French politician Louis d'Orléans lamented in 1594 that it was simply impossible to know the true identity of the dissimulator.[28]

I have suggested that some information in *La mancata fede* just cited could have been provided in spoken asides. Whether these asides were made directly to the audience or not cannot be determined. Richard Andrews demonstrates that in the learned comedy, which commedia dell'arte imitated, Aelius Donatus's fourth-century prohibition against direct address to the audience was not strictly followed (1988, pp. 153–168). But the only clear indications of acknowledgments of the audience in the Scala scenarios are when in Day 26, *Li tappeti alessandrini*, Pantalone's bows to everyone ["*facendo riverenza al popolo*"] but no one is left on stage except himself, (II, 263)[29] and, similarly, in Day 37, *La caccia*, where Scala tells us that the Captain, alone on stage, "bows to the people" ["*fa riverenza al popolo*"], and, with more certain reference to the audience, says, " 'May it do you good, Ladies and Gentlemen,' and exits" (II, 381). Whether the humor came from the shock of such infrequent breaks though the proscenium wall or whether such breaks were a regular occurrence, particularly in the asides and in the frequent soliloquies, thus providing regular intimacy between character and audience, is not easy to determine.

In many instances, emotions had to have been shown for the benefit of the audience when there was no opportunity for spoken asides. The reactions had to have been conveyed entirely by facial and bodily means. This is most often evident in situations were when one character, often at a window, overhears events in the street below without those in the street knowing. In the first act of Day 19, *Li tre fidi amici*, Isabella "at the window shows that she has heard everything" (I, 198). In the same scenario, Flaminia, at the window, "has heard Flavio say he is going to leave, and grief-stricken, she bites her finger and withdraws weeping" (1, 197). In this latter instance, we are told explicitly how Flaminia reacts to what she overhears. In Day 11, *Il capitano*, Isabella, also at the window, "hears everything and shows by gestures that she is in a rage" (I, 123). In Day 23, *Il portalettere*, Flavio and Orazio each "makes signs" of their love to their loved ones at windows above (II, 235). In the same scenario, Orazio, "beside himself and all impassioned departs in silence" (II, 233). In Day 1, *Li duo vecchi gemelli,* the old bawd and would-be sorceress, Pasquella, conjures up someone who then actually appears. She "is amazed at this knowing that she really knows nothing about magic at all, and begins to tremble with fear" (I, 20). So listening, grief, fury, love, madness, amazement, and fear, all, on occasion, needed to have been conveyed wordlessly. There are even harder challenges for wordless communication: in Day 27, *La mancata fede*, Burratino, having been convinced that if he speaks within a three-day period he will be possessed by demons, with gestures "indicates [in terror] that these [people who come into the piazza] are all demons" (II, 280).

Emotions and resultant actions are frequently sudden: when Burattino, in the excerpts from *La mancata fede* provided at the onset, sees a girl disguised as a pilgrim whom he mistakenly takes to be lower class like himself, he immediately makes passes at her and then attempts to kiss her. In another scene in the same act, Orazio bursts into tears. Isabella then suddenly starts weeping too. Sword fights erupt with the least provocation.

Characters can also immediately change emotions. Cicero and Quintilian, both highly influential on the rhetoric of the period, believed that in real life one could suddenly be overcome by a violent passion and that it could then change quickly (Doran, 1954, pp. 235–236). These views may well have influenced the representation of passions in drama. In the third act of Day 14, *Il pellegrino fido amante* the lover, Flavio, disguised as a pilgrim, enters weeping over the death of Isabella, whom he refers to by name. Hearing of her death, the Doctor, her father, falls to the ground as if dead. Fabrizio, who is actually Isabella disguised as a page, enters, sees her lover, Flavio, and rejoices. But, then, she immediately sees her father lying as if dead and begins to weep. At this point, the Doctor regains consciousness. Isabella falls to her knees and, begging forgiveness, identifies herself. As they embrace, the pilgrim reveals himself to be Flavio and all rejoice. Whether or not such changes were understood as realistic, they called attention to the skill of the actors. Rapid emotional changes, evident throughout Scala's scenarios, to judge by their frequency, were much enjoyed by audiences.[30]

Thus far, we have seen the ways in which emotional responses were conveyed not only through speech but also through considerable and legible gesture. The relationship between actor and audience was intimate, as, perhaps, in direct address to the audience, was the relationship between character and audience. The disguises, the strong emotions, and the rapid changes between them, along with the improvisation and seeming improvisation from more or less set material that characterized much of commedia dell'arte performance called attention to the acting as acting and elicited audience appreciation for it. The frequent use of disguised characters suggests both the pleasure the audience had in being privy to the deception but also their pleasure in its effectiveness. They could see how the disguises could be persuasive.

The unfamiliarity with Italian Renaissance culture may also lead us to read all characters, with or without disguises as merely stereotypes and caricatures: as the braggart warrior, the foolish old men, the wayward children, and the wily or lazy servants. They were that. But the relationships between the characters also epitomize real tensions within the society: between citizens and society; fathers and sons; female lovers, wives, and widows and men; lovers; friends; citizens and servants; and with outsiders. And thus, like the magicians and ghosts, their representations are far more real for Renaissance viewers than has been acknowledged. The captain stands in variously for both the resented Spanish who dominated much of Italy and for the much reviled mercenary soldiers whose infamous reputation lived on, blamed, as they were, for the earlier seizure of Italy by the French.[31] Women's sexuality, uncontrolled, because women naturally lack reason and have very strong sex drives, could destroy the family honor and lineage; youths, yet lacking in adult reason, could dissipate the family fortune; and the lower classes, who naturally followed their baser instincts, could trick their betters in any number of ways, and this habit of social inversion hinted at social revolution (Trexler, 1980, pp. 16, 367). Adult male citizens, if guided by passion, could themselves disrupt the social order. In each of the character interactions real societal anxieties were expressed.

I develop this idea here with but a single example. In Day 25, *La gelosa Isabella*, the title character, on the basis of a single misunderstood incident, becomes so jealous because of the behavior of her lover, Orazio, that, disguised as a man, she seeks to kill him in a duel. From her window, on what is pretty surely a night of Carnival, Isabella sees Orazio, as she supposes, propositioning a maidservant.

To the other characters accompanying them at the time and to the audience, it is clear that Orazio, in the spirit of Carnival, is just joking around. Isabella's jealousy and the revenge she seeks may thus seem merely irrational, an excuse for highly theatrical antics. But given the mores of the time, they are also finely motivated, the psychology well-observed, and calling for more nuanced acting than may be apparent. Orazio, whom Isabella sees propositioning the maidservant, is arriving late for his secret rendezvous with Isabella under cover of night, she at her window and he beneath it. Isabella much anticipates this meeting and, as Scala tells us, is worried that Orazio is so late. She is, as the innkeeper implies, filled with the strong uncontrollable sexual passion young girls were thought to have. On this account, she lives confined within her father's house, her virginity protected so that his house is not dishonored and her offspring legitimate and conceived with a man of her father's choosing. As if to emphasize the frustration for Isabella of her confinement, Scala keeps her in the house until Act II, Scene 12. Orazio's seeming pass at a maidservant right beneath her window as she awaits his visit makes her envious and dishonors her. What is more, the maidservant is accompanying a girl of Isabella's own middling-elite social class, whose evidently more liberal father has allowed her out of the house to partake in Carnival. To make matters worse, awaiting Orazio's arrival, Isabella has just seen her father in the street off to a party and interested in the offer of an innkeeper to find him a courtesan. Such interest was not appropriate for a patriarch; as the innkeeper later explains, " 'when fathers have bad habits it often causes the ruin of their daughters' " (II, 254). Isabella is left trapped within upholding the honor of the house while her father himself dishonors it. The maidservant proceeds to further dishonor Isabella by talking back to her when Isabella accuses her and then by playing a trick on her.

Thus, Scala amply motivates Isabella's seemingly irrational behavior. The conflicts between sexual passion and honor are variously explored. The cultural divide of four hundred years may make it easy to fail to notice that Isabella's motivation is more complex, deeper, and more genuine than we might at first think. The scenarios, while they call for broad acting, at the same time require considerable subtlety. Incidentally, for Renaissance viewers, Isabella's quick temper and her jealousy revealed the depth of her love (Crane, 1971, pp. 35, 143). We might miss that too.

While the acting was in general broad and the gestures relatively fixed so that they could be read and designed to remind us that we were in a theatre, at the same time, they could also be subtle and they did not seem as unrealistic to their audiences as they seem to us today.

******

From Quintilian's teaching on oration we can pretty reliably infer a great deal about the actor's use of voice. Wilbourne's work on voice causes us to regard Quintilian's words on voice and the brief descriptions of voice in writing about commedia dell'arte at the time of its performance as descriptions of something considerably more musical and less like ordinary speech than has been previously supposed. The sound of the voice, like gesture, was specific to class, sex, age, regionality, occupation, and emotional state.

The visual record of commedia dell'arte performance in the period is an important aid in the study of gesture. Bevington has usefully pointed to the general belief in the humors and the defined physical manifestations following from them. Quintilian indicates how gesture is used in the expression of ideas and he shows that gesture can be learned, routinized, and accordingly widely recognized. Our familiarity with many of the gestures in the historical record suggests that many gestures may be more widespread and perhaps enduring than particular languages. But the work of Morris, et al. leads to caution in making generalizations in this respect. Scala is a useful and reliable guide to gesture in commedia dell'arte. But because his scenarios provide almost no speech, they cannot tell us much about the correlation between speech and gesture or about the expression of ideas through gesture. Taken together, Bevington's work, Quintilian, and Scala's scenarios suggest that gestures were numerous and, from our perspective, immoderate.

An understanding of the specificity of the use of voice and of gesture serve to refine our understanding of the comprehension of characters' use of dialects.

Notes

1 Scala's collection is available in a modern edition in Italian (Scala, Marotti, 1976). Thirty of the scenarios are available in English (Scala, Andrews, 2008), and all fifty are available in English in a somewhat unreliable translation (Scala, Salero, 1967).
2 The primary source for speeches and dialogs remains Vito Pandolfi's, *La commedia dell'arte: storia e testi,* (6 vols.), vols. 1–5, (1957–1961).
3 Erith Jaffe-Berg's ambitious *The Multilingual Art of Commedia dell'Arte* (2009) takes on performance from the sixteenth through the twentieth centuries. It is, as she explains, "not an historic account of multilingualism in commedia dell'arte but rather, a more theoretical study of language, multilingualism and its function in *commedia dell'arte*" (p. 31).
4 All page references to Clivio are from his 1989 essay.
5 It was taught to males. Females had no place in public life and for them silence was a virtue. The eloquence of women in commedia dell'arte must be the more admired
6 Quintilian was "the revered authority behind every humanistic pedagogical treatise" (Grendler, 1989, p. 120).
7 All further references to Quintilian are to this edition, book 11 of Quintilian.
8 To make clear the power of delivery, Quintilian, paraphrasing Cicero, claims

> that when Demosthenes was asked what the most important thing in the whole business of oratory was, he gave the prize to Delivery, and he gave it the second and the third place too, until they stopped asking; we must therefore suppose that he thought of it not just as the first faculty needed, but as the only one
> (Quintilian, 2001, pp. 87, 89; (Cicero, [55 BCE] 1977, p. 169).

However, Quintilian himself, who revered the orations of Cicero, did not endorse the view that the words did not matter and Cicero, even today, is famous for his orations – in writing.
9 I infer that public speaking for those who went to vernacular schools was not important; students in these schools would not have been trained for law, medicine, teaching, or the clergy.
10 All page references to Wilbourne in this section are to Wilbourne (2016).

11 Similarly the words on voice by actor, playwright, and director Leoni de'Sommi (c. 1565) and poet and dramatist Angelo Ingegneri (1594), both advising on written drama, rather than improvised, must gain new interest following Wilbourne's focus on Galilei. Both tell us that word, voice, and gesture are to form a unity designed to convey the emotional state of the characters represented. And they should all be in accord with nature. It is pretty clear, however, that this nature is to be theatrically enhanced: the voice, as important as gesture, should be unlike ordinary speech in being louder and slower, the words more clearly pronounced, and more melodic (de Sommi, [1556] 1968, pp. 40–41; Ingegneri, (1594] 1989), pp. 30–31).

12 One can hear a recitative both spoken and sung, quite outside the historical context presented in Wilbourne, in a lecture-demonstration provided by Claudia Friedlander on YouTube called "How to Sing Recitative" (accessed, July 25, 2018) In it, it should be said, no claim is made that the singer provides either a "perfect" recitation or recitative.

13 Ludovico Dolce (1560) analogized an unmarried girl's body to " 'a ship floating in a sea of many dangers, all the orifices of which have to be closed so that these dangers cannot penetrate into the inner parts' " (Gordon, 2006, p. 188).

14 Peter Burke remarks upon variations in what he calls the "domains of gesture": family, court, church, etc. (2004, p. 75).

15 Meredith Chilton (2001), working with porcelain sculptures of commedia dell'arte figures from over a hundred years later than the period I consider, skillfully analyzes gestures in these then popular porcelain figurines.

16 Bonifaccio, as his title suggests, includes not only gestures but signs, including physiognomical characteristics and such things as a "fog around the head" which presages death (1616, p. 32).

17 Julia Sutton's 1995 English translation and edition of *Nobiltà di dame* enhances Caroso's work by adding explanations of dance terms, a discussion of notes on style and advice on learning the steps, the relationships between music and dance, and a Labanotation manual of dance step-types for those wishing to reconstruct various of the dances.

18 Interestingly, the Italian dancing masters also taught riding and fencing: three arts that befit a gentleman.

19 This editorial clarification is provided by Sutton.

20 Sometimes it is explained that this was so because the left hand was occupied holding up the toga. Perhaps. But the same recommendation appears in eighteenth-century books on rhetoric.

21 Less persuasively, Buckley goes on to argue that the woodcuts show a four-act dramatic progression of images from left to right, act by act. He claims that there was a relationship between the progression of images he sees and virtually choreographed commedia performance, and that, at least some of the images represent emblematic visual tableaux present in performance, static moments held for effect during which audience members not understanding the language could read the significance of the particular episode (p. 263). For the fraught discussion of the appropriate inclusion and ordering of the images in the Recueil Fossard album see M. A. Katritzsky (2008, pp. 108-114). For Buckley's views on this see Buckley (2009, fn. 28, p. 313).

22 This section on Scala's scenarios is, in the main, a somewhat cut version of my essay on the topic (Schmitt, 2012), which appeared in *New Theatre Quarterly* vol. 28, 4 (2012), pp. 325-333. Reprinted with permission of Cambridge University Press.

23 I demonstrate the possibility of such reconstructions in my *Befriending the Commedia dell'Arte of Flaminios Scala* (2014).

24 M.A. Katritzky (2006) has observed that a significant number of early upper-class female characters are depicted in the iconography with faces either wholly or partially covered by a veil or mask (pp. 202–204). These seem to have served for propriety rather than as character masks

25 Scala provides brief examples of mad speech in Day 38, *La pazzia d'Isabella*. For the use of song in the representation of madness, see Anne MacNeil (2003, p. 49).
26 In Canto 29: "From the moment he was possessed by madness he had always gone naked." Nudity had been part of the folklore of madness for a long time.
27 Conversely, sumptuary law forbade people from dressing above their station. And they almost never disguise themselves as characters above their station in Scala.
28 From *Le Banquet ou aprés-dinée du comte d'Arète,* as cited in Snyder (2009, p. xiv).
29 All references in parentheses are to the volume and page number in Flaminio Scala ([1611] 1976). Scala, probably following Boccaccio, whose tales were often used in commedia dell'arte, numbered his fifty scenarios by days.
30 The rapid emotional changes were probably also present in scenes of madness. In his *Anatomy of Melancholy* ([1624] 1964), Robert Burton (Burton ([1628] 1964, vol. 1, pp. 389, 394) suggests that those afflicted with madness experience rapid mood changes and sometimes think they hear and see phantasms, the visions of which would lead to such rapid emotional changes. In a mad speech written by Isabella Andreini, the character responds to such various phantasms.
31 See for instance, Niccolò Machiavelli, *The Prince* (1532), chapter 12.

Works cited

Andrews, Richard. (1988). "Rhetoric and Drama: Monologues and Set Speeches in Aretino's Comedies." In *The Languages of Literature in Renaissance Italy*, edited by Peter Hainsworth, Valerio Lucchesi, Christina Roaf, David Robey, and J.R. Woodhouse, pp. 153–168. (Oxford: Clarendon Press).

Andrews, Richard. (2008). *The Commedia dell'Arte of Flaminio Scala: A Translation and Analysis of 30 Scenarios*. Edited and translated by Richard Andrews. (Plymouth, UK: Scarecrow Press).

Barasch, Moshe. (1976). *Gestures of Despair in Medieval and Early Renaissance Art*. (New York: New York University Press).

Bevington, David. (1984). *Action is Eloquence: Shakespeare's Language of Gesture*. (Cambridge, MA: Harvard University Press).

Biow, Douglas. (2010). "The Beard in Sixteenth-Century Italy." In *The Body in Early Modern Italy*, edited by Julia L. Hairston and Walter Stephens, pp. 176–194. (Baltimore, MD: Johns Hopkins University Press).

Bonifaccio, Giovanni. (1616). *L'arte de' Cenni. . . .* (Venice: Francesco Grossi). Available on Google Books.

Boughner, Daniel C. (1954). *The Braggart in Renaissance Comedy: A Study in Comparative Drama from Aristophanes to Shakespeare*. (Minneapolis: University of Minnesota Press).

Buckley, Matthew. (2009) "Eloquent Action: The Body and Meaning in Early Commedia Dell'Arte." *Theatre Survey* 50, 2: pp. 251-316.

Burke, Peter. (1992). "The Language of Gesture in Early Modern Italy." In *A Cultural History of Gesture*, edited by Jan Bremmer and Herman Roodenburg, pp. 71–83. (Cambridge, UK: Polity).

Burke, Peter. (2004). *Language and Communities in Early Modern Europe*, vol. 1. (Cambridge: Cambridge University Press).

Burton, Robert. (1964). *The Anatomy of Melancholy*. (3 vols). (New York: Everyman's Library).

Carlson, Marvin. (2006). *Speaking in Tongues: Language at Play in the Theatre*. (Ann Arbor: University of Michigan).

Caroso, Fabrizio. ([1600] 1995). *Courtly Dance of the Renaissance A New Translation and Edition of the Nobilta di Dame* 1600. Translated and edited by Julia Sutton with music and commentary by F. Marian Walker. (Mineola, NY: Dover).

Castiglione, Baldesar. ([1967] 1976). *The Book of the Courtier*. Translated by George Bull. Introduction by George Bull, pp. xxvi–xxviii. (Baltimore, MD: Penguin Publishing).

Cecchini, Pier Maria (1991). "Discorso sopra l'arte comic co il modo di ben recitare" In Ferruccio Marotti and Giovanni Romei. (1994) *La commedia dell'arte e la società barocca: La professione del teatro*. vol. 2 (Rome: Bulzoni) 67-76.

Chilton, Meredith. (2001). *Harlequin Unmasked: The Commedia dell'Arte and Porcelain Sculpture*. (New Haven, CT: The George R. Gardiner Museum of Ceramic Art with Yale University Press).

Cicero. ([c. 80s, 90s BCE] 1954). *Ad C. Herennium de ratione diceni: Rhetorica ad Herennium*. Loeb Classical Library. Translated by Harry Caplan. (Cambridge, MA: Harvard University Press).

Cicero. ([55 BCE] 1977). *De oratore*, Book III. (28 vols). Translated by H. Rackham. (Cambridge, MA: Harvard University Press).

Clivio, Gianrenzo P. (1989). "The Languages of the *commedia dell'arte*." In *The Science of Buffoonery: Theory and History of the Commedia dell'Arte*, edited by Domenico Pietropaolo, pp. 209–237. (Ottawa, ON: Dovehouse Editions).

Crane, Thomas Frederick. (1971). *Italian Social Customs of the Sixteenth Century and Their Influence on the Literatures of Europe*. (New York: Russell and Russell).

de Jorio, Andrea. ([1832] 2000). *La mimica degli antichi investigata nel gestire napoletano. [Gestural Expression of the Ancients in the Light of Neapolitan Gesturing]*. Translated by Adam Kendon. (Bloomington: Indiana University Press).

de'Sommi, Leone. (1968). *Quattro dialoghi in material di rappresentazioni sceniche*. (Milan: Il Polifilo).

Doran, Madeleine. (1954). *Endeavors of Art: A Study of Form in Elizabethan Drama*. (Madison: University of Wisconsin Press).

Fitzpatrick, Tim. (1995). *The Relationship of Oral and Literate Performance Processes in the Commedia dell'Arte: Beyond the Improvisation/Memorisation Divide*. (Lewiston, NY: Edwin Mellen Press).

Galli, Quirino (2005). *Gli scenari di Flaminio Scala: Lingua e teoria teatrale*. (Salerno: Pietro Laveglia).

Gordon, Bonnie. (2006). "The Courtesan's Singing Body as Cultural Capital in Seventeenth-Century Italy." In *The Courtesan's Arts: Cross-Cultural Perspectives*, edited by Martha Feldman and Bonnie Gordon, pp. 182–208. (Oxford: Oxford University Press).

Grendler, Paul. (1989). *Schooling in Renaissance Italy: Literacy and Learning, 1300–1600*. (Baltimore, MD: Johns Hopkins University Press).

Henke, Robert. (2002). *Performance and Literature in the Commedia dell'Arte*. (Cambridge: Cambridge University Press).

Hulfeld, Stefan. (2014). *Scenari più scelti d'istrioni: Italienisch-Deutsche Edition der einhundert Commedia all'improvviso – Szenarien aus der Sammlung Corsiniana*. (2 vols.) (Göttingen: DE, V&R unipress).

Ingegneri, Angelo. (1989). *Della poesia rappresentativa*. (Ferrara: Instituto di Studi Rinascimentali).

Jaffe-Berg, Erith. (2009). *The Multilingual Art of Commedia dell'Arte*. (Toronto, ON: Legas).

Karim-Cooper, Farah. (2016). *The Hand on the Shakespearean Stage: Gesture, Touch, and the Spectacle of Dismemberment*. (London: Bloomsbury).

Katritzky, M.A. (1989). "The Recueil Fossard 1928-88: a review and three reconstructions. In: Cairns, Christophe ed. *The Commedia dell'arte from the Renassance to Dario Fo: The Italian Origins of European Theatre*. v.6, pp. 99-116. (Lewiston ME: Edward Mellen Press).

Katritzky, M.A. (2006). *The Art of Commedia: A Study in the Commedia dell'Arte 1560–1620 with Special Reference to the Visual Records*. (Amsterdam: Rodopi).

Kendon, Adam. (2000). Introduction to *Gesture in Naples and Gesture in Classical Antiquity*, a translation of Andrea de Jorio, *La mimica degli antichi investigata nel gestire napoletano/Gestural Expression of the Ancients in the Light of Neapolitan Gesturing* Translation by Adam Kendon. (Bloomington: Indiana University Press).

Kendon, Adam. (2004). *Gesture: Visible Action as Utterance*. (Cambridge: Cambridge University Press).

Knox, Dilwyn. (1991). "Giovanni Bonifaccio. *L'arte de cenni* and Renaissance Ideas of Gesture." In *Italia ed Europa nella linguistica del Rinascimento: confronti e relatiazioni: atti del convegno international*, vol 2, edited by Mirko Tavoni, pp. 379–400. (Moderna: F.C. Panini).

Knox, Dilwyn. (2000). "Civility, Courtesy and Women." In *Women in Italian Renaissance Culture and Society*, edited by Letizia Panizza, pp. 2–17. (Oxford: University of Oxford).

Lea, K.M. ([1934] 1962). *Italian Popular Comedy: A Study in the Commedia dell'Arte, 1560–1620 with Special Reference to the English Stage*, vol. 2. (2 vols). (New York: Russell & Russell).

Mack, Peter. (2011). *A History of Renaissance Rhetoric 1380–1620*. (Oxford: Oxford University Press).

MacNeil, Anne. (2003). *Music and Women of the Commedia dell'Arte in the Late Sixteenth Century*. (Oxford: Oxford University Press).

Marotti, Ferruccio and Giovanna Romei. (1991). *La commedia dell'arte e la società barocca: La professione del teatro*. (Rome: Bulzoni).

Morris, Desmond, Peter Collett, Peter Marsh, and Marie O'Shaugnessy. (1979). *Gestures: Their Origins and Distribution*. (New York: Stein and Day).

Murphy, James J. (1983) *Renaissance Eloquence: Studies in the Theory and Practice of Renaissance Rhetoric*. (Berkeley, CA: Universituy of California Press).

Perrucci, Andrea. ([1699] 2008). *Dell'arte rappresentative premeditate, ed all'improvviso*. Bilingual edition in English and Italian. Translated and edited by Francesco Cotticelli, Anne Goodrich Heck, and Thomas F. Heck. (Lanham, MD: Scarecrow Press).

Quintilian, Marcus Fabian. (2001). *The Orator's Education: Books 11–12*, vol. 5. Edited and translated by Donald A. Russell. (Cambridge, MA: Harvard University Press).

Roodenburg, Herman. (1992). "The Hand of Friendship." In *A Cultural History of Gesture*, edited by Jan N. Bremmer and Herman Roodenburg, pp. 152–189. (Ithaca, NY: Cornell University Press).

Ruggiero, Laura Giannetti (née Laura Giannetti). (2005). "When Male Characters Pass as Women: Theatrical Play and Social Practice in the Italian Renaissance." *Sixteenth Century Journal* 36 (3): pp. 743-760).

Salkeld, Duncan. (1993). *Madness and Drama in the Age of Shakespeare*. (Manchester, UK: Manchester University Press).

Scala, Flaminio. ([1611] 1976). *Il teatro delle favole rappresentative*, vol. 1. (2 vols). Edited by Ferruccio Marotti. (Milan: Il Polifilo).

Schmitt, Natalie Crohn. (2012). "The Style of Commedia dell'Arte Acting: Observations Drawn from the Scenarios of Flaminio Scala." *New Theatre Quarterly* 28 (4): pp. 325–333.

Schmitt, Natalie Crohn. (2014). *Befriending the Commedia dell'Arte of Flaminios Scala.* (Toronto, ON: University of Toronto Press).

Sloane, Thomas O. (1997). *On the Contrary: The Protocol of Traditional Rhetoric.* (Washington DC: Catholic University Press).

Snyder, Jon. R. (2009). *Dissimulation and the Culture of Secrecy in Early Modern Europe.* (Berkeley: University of California Press).

Sutton, Julia. (1991). *Il Ballarino: The Art of Renaissance Danc*e. Demonstration narrated by Julia Sutton. DVD. (Pennington, NJ: Dance Horizons, Princeton Book Company).

Sutton, Julia. (1995). *Courtly Dance of the Renaissance: a new translation and edition of the Nobilta di dame*, 1600. Translated and edited by Julia Sutton with music and commentary by F. Marian Walker. See especially chapters 3 and 4. (Mineola, NY: Dover).

Tessari, Roberto (1981). *Commedia dell'arte: la maschere e l'ombra.* (Milan: Mursia)

Trexler, Richard C. (1980). *Public Life in Renaissance Florence.* (New York: Academic Press).

Tunstall, Darren. (2016). *Shakespeare and Gesture in Practice.* (New York: Palgrave).

Valesio, Paolo. (1971). "The Language of Madness in the Renaissance." *Yearbook of Italian Studies* 1: pp. 199–234.

Vickers, Brian. (1988). *In Defence of Rhetoric.* (Oxford: Clarendon Press).

Wilbourne, Emily. (2016) *Seventeenth-Century Opera and the Sound of the Commedia dell'Arte.* (Chicago, IL: University of Chicago Press).

3 The uses of masks

In this chapter, I try to explain why, throughout its history, the commedia dell'arte actors persisted in wearing masks. The chapter falls into two parts. 1. Character masks. These masks (Pantalone, and Harlequin, are examples) are best known from the majority of the scenarios, the comedies, but they were also employed in the tragedies and pastorals and in genre combinations. Rather than focus on descriptions of these masks, frequently described elsewhere, the chapter examines their function. 2. Other masks. This broad category includes personifications of allegorical figures, classical gods, devils and spirits, animals, and character masks temporarily transformed into animals, trees, fountains, and stones. The majority of these masks are restricted to pastorals and tragicomedies.

Surprisingly, with all the attention given the character masks, masking specific to the pastorals and tragicomedies has not been examined. It is, to be sure, the character masks, particularly as they appear in the comedies that are the most important to commedia dell'arte. They appear in almost all the scenarios from which the performers worked. I therefore address them first.

I limit my study to consideration of three scenario collections, all from the period when commedia dell'arte was at its height, in the latter part of the sixteenth century and the first part of the seventeenth century. Only one of these collections, that of the fifty scenarios by Flaminio Scala in 1611, was published.[1] The Corsini collection of one hundred scenarios is believed to have been written down in manuscript form between 1600 and 1615.[2] The Locatelli collection's 103 scenarios, also in manuscript form, were bound together in two volumes, one in 1618 and the other in 1622.[3] The Corsini and the more detailed Locatelli collection are both thought to be records of, in many cases, very similar performances having circulated in Rome between 1570 and 1613 (Hulfeld, 2014, p. 54). Taken together, the three collections constitute about a third of the total known scenarios. I work from the fifty scenarios in the Scala collection made available in modern print editions: the thirty Locatelli scenarios available in print (Lea, [1934] 1962, pp. 555–674; Testaverde, 2007, pp. 178–424); and the one hundred scenarios in the Corsini collection recently made available in an excellent print edition with color reproductions of its original watercolors (Hulfeld, 2014). Uniquely, the Corsini collection contains watercolor illustrations, one prefacing each scenario in the collection. Stefano Mengarelli gives the date of the paintings as sometime

Table 3.1 Breakdown of genre types: Corsini, Scala, Locatelli.

	Comedies	*Tragedies*	*Pastorals*	*Tragicomedies*	*Other*
Corsini:					
100 scenarios	75	1	11	10	3
Scala:					
50 scenarios	40	1	1		8
Locatelli:					
103 scenarios	80	2	8	12	1

around 1625 and 1638, that is, some while after after the estimated dates of the scenario transcriptions: 1600-1615 (cited in Hulfeld, 2014, p. 50).

To have included scenarios of later or less certain dates would have greatly complicated my efforts, particularly because advances in theatre technology seem often to have resulted in scenarios with frequent set changes, sometimes for every scene, and including interior scenes,[4] so that the general relationship for which I argue between setting, genre, and the kinds of masks employed seemed difficult or impossible to apply.

Under "other" (listed in Table 3.1 above) fall various experimental genres: in Corsini, two Turkish dramas and one royal drama; in Scala, one mixed drama, four royal dramas (one of these taking up three scenarios), and one heroic drama; and in Locatelli: one heroic drama. As we shall see in the next section of this essay, any count of scenarios by genre type can be somewhat misleading: generalities about the kinds of characters and figures that may appear respectively in them have exceptions. Further, assumptions about the relative popularity of scenarios by genre type one might be tempted to make are not altogether as clear as it might seem.

Character masks in commedia dell'arte

In Latin, "*persona*" is the word for mask, especially as worn by an actor. In the Roman theatre, the term "mask" was used to apply not only to the mask but also to the masked character. So, too, in discussing commedia dell'arte, "mask" can refer to the mask the actor wore or to the character he or she mostly played. Some characters in commedia dell'arte were routinely masked, others were not, but both are commonly referred to as "masks."

Comedies focus on the masks of those from the middle and lower classes of urban society. The actually masked stock characters, the *parti ridiculi*, or funny roles, always male, included the *vecchi* or middle-class citizens and the *zanni*, usually their servants, but sometimes innkeepers, or other lower-class characters, not citizens, and a captain, usually representative of a *condottiero*, a mercenary, hired to fight in the wars between the city-states or of one of the resented Spaniards occupying large parts of the Italian peninsula, in either case, a braggart warrior.

If these characters sound familiar from Roman drama that is because the earlier *commedia erudita*, or learned comedy, was based on classical drama. Roman drama; with some modifications – servants for the most part instead of slaves, for instance – served equally as well to represent the Italian Renaissance middle class, their families, and servants. So, the commedia dell'arte could profitably take these characters for their own use. In exaggerated form, the scenarios mirrored people in urban Renaissance life. They struck a respondent chord with their audience.

There is no evidence that *commedia erudita* employed masks; commedia dell'arte did. But unlike the masks in ancient theatre, the comic commedia dell'arte masks, the ones with which we are familiar, left the mouth free for facial expression and they were made of leather, rather than linen, a material closer to animal and human. David Wiles suggests that they liberated non-civilized behavior (Wiles, 1991, p. 126). Their actual origin is unknown. Enrico Fulchignoni argues that their origin is Middle-Eastern (Fulchignoni, 1990). The more immediate influence may have been the carnival masks used in the pre-Lenten revelry throughout Italy and in many other, particularly southern, European countries, although those masks tended to be full-faced.

Domenico Pietropaolo states that Harlequin masks remaining to us from sometime in the seventeenth and eighteenth centuries would have been set at a distance from the face like glasses and from these remaining masks he conjectures that this distance from the face, together with the masks' small eyeholes, would have required the actor to constantly move his head from side to side and up and down in order to see (Pietropaolo, 2001, p. 23). Pantalone's slippers would have obliged him to walk other than if he had been wearing boots and a sword like the captain. So, there was an interaction between the mask, considered largely as the character's aspect, and the characterization.

Unmasked characters – the upper-class lovers, the *innamorati*, male and female, and the lower-class female servants – are also referred to as "masks." Their presence onstage not only enlarged and strengthened the roles of female characters in drama and, in the case of the lovers, the romantic and lyrical aspects of the drama as well, but also the presence of actresses, in themselves, particularly unmasked, must have greatly enhanced the popularity of the theatre and its interest for both female and male audience members.[5] Scala's Day 39, "*Il ritratto*" is specifically about husbands lost to the theatre because of their adoration of its leading lady. Needless to say, the presence of women in the female roles, particularly in roles of ladies, outraged Church fathers and violated the social constraints against women's appearance in public and onstage.

Like the masked characters, characters with no masks displayed a kind of clothing, manner, and dialect that made them readily identifiable even when the scenario required them to behave in ways in which we had not previously seen them behave. Thus, Richard Andrews describes a mask as "a fixed role with a fixed name, transferable from one play to another, delineated by external characteristics which did not change - these including most crucially, a characteristic verbal delivery, incorporating a recognizable social accent or regional vernacular" (Andrews, 2008, p. xx). As James Johnson puts it, "the masks served to preserve identities, to hold their characters consistent even as particular plots place them in different occupations and family configurations" (Johnson, 2011, p. 75).

Louise George Clubb perhaps best describes the character mask as a "semi-fixed" role (Clubb, 1989, p. 19).[6] For instance, the identity of both the masked *zanni*, usually a servant, and of the unmasked *innamorata* could be readily identified even though the role assignments for their masks might vary considerably from scenario to scenario. In the scenarios of Flaminio Scala the *zanni* Burattino is utilized as a servant, an innkeeper, a beggar, a peasant, a postman, a patient father, or a clueless husband. He is sometimes perceptive, sometimes not. The unmasked *innamorata* is variously vengefully jealous, a very undutiful daughter, an adulterous wife, a devoted lover, an astrologer, a witless girl, or a very smart plot-manipulator. She could travel great distances; she could remain at home; she could feign madness or be actually mad. She could sing, dance, and convincingly disguise herself as a gypsy, a manservant, a young gentleman, or a French-speaking widow. Beneath it all she had the manners and usually the costume of an upper-class woman and she spoke Tuscan, the literary language (and that of Petrarch), which, in the case of the most famous *innamorata* Isabella Andreini, she was known to incorporate into her own. The masked and unmasked characters were, like the actor Charlie Chaplin, instantly identifiable no matter the role.[7]

Masks and unmasked characters could mix freely on the stage because in some sense there was no difference between them. Peter Brook observed that what he calls a "traditional mask," is "a portrait of a man without a mask . . . an outer casting that is a complete and sensitive reflection of the inner life" (Brook, 1987, pp. 218, 231). The mask served "not to hide the character but expose it." The contemporary mask-maker and commedia performer Antonio Fava makes essentially the same point about the commedia mask: "the character externalizes everything" (Fava, 2007, p. 136).

The inner life of the mask was plain for the audience and the other characters to see, but not for the character himself. The French maxim writer François de la Rochefoucauld, 1613–1680, remarked that "it is as easy to deceive ourselves without knowing as it is hard to deceive others without their finding it out" (cited in Barish, 1981, p. 213). The inability of the old men to see themselves for what they were led to their humiliation and downfall. Pantalone was always hopelessly unaware of the absurdity of his inappropriate sexual advances. His obliviousness and consequent unseemly behavior led to his comeuppance.

The comedies rely on a relatively fixed set of characters: two *vecchi* (old men), Pantalone and Graziano; two, sometimes three, male *zanni*; two sets of young lovers, male and female; and a captain. Sometimes they call for extra characters: a female servant, a messenger, a hangman, a footman, a Turk, a mountebank, slaves, musicians. The rare additional female, usually a mother, would not have been masked. We do not know whether the more comic additional characters were masked or not. M.A. Katritzsky believes that the additional *vecchi*, a Frenchman in the frontispiece to the Corsini II/34 "Li porci" is masked (Katritzky, 2006, p. 166). Each mask, like its requisite costume, would have entailed added expense and baggage for the mostly vagabond players. On the other hand, it would seem logical, in keeping with the regular comic characters, that they were masked, particularly if the actor playing them was required to play another role or roles as well. Slaves, when they appear in the watercolors preceding each of the Corsini scenarios are defined by their attribute, a slave collar, Turks by their short gowns and turbans. It should be said that the relationship between the illustrations provided as the frontispiece for each scenario in the Corsini manuscript and performance of the scenarios varies and they are not altogether reliable guides to their performance (Mengarelli, 2014). They are, nonetheless, very helpful.

Performers left no known explanation for why they wore masks. There were widespread clerical denunciations of the wearing of masks both by the general populace during Carnival and by performers in the commedia dell'arte. Tomaso Garzoni, a member of the Order of Latern Canons in Ravenna, wrote in 1585 that masks were the visible remnant of original sin: "the first mask ever to be seen on the face of the earth, was without doubt the dark angel, who, in the guise of the malicious serpent, seduced our first mother to horrible excess" (cited in Johnson, 2011, p. 79). Specifically of masks in the commedia dell'arte, the archbishop of Milan, Charles Borromeo wrote in 1572, that they were "abominable." Behind them "it becomes licit for men to utter filthy and dishonest words, to make lewd gestures and commit immodest acts! Wicked mask, impugner of honesty, inimical to gravity, ruin of every charge the Christian soul must keep within and without" (cited in Johnson, 2011, p. 73). Andrea Perrucci, who theorized about commedia dell'arte contemporary with its performance (in 1699) tells us only that "in comedy I deem the ridiculous mask not only appropriate, but also necessary, because it induces laughter" (Perrucci, [1699] 2008, p. 22). So firmly established were character masks that they are never mentioned in any of the prop lists or in the scenarios themselves. Each character actor had his own. Their use was simply a given.

Utility of character masks for the actors

From archbishop Borromeo's condemnation we can infer something of the attraction of masks for actors: they allowed actors to say things and behave in ways that they could not in their person. They could break the social hierarchy and sexual taboos, deceive, lie, and escape the consequences. Cultural historian James H. Johnson cites Tristano Martinelli, who occasionally signed his letters not as Martinelli but as Arlecchino, the *zanni* he played. In that persona he addressed Grand Duke Ferdinanda de' Medici as the "highest master of footgear," Ferdinanda Gonzaga, Duke of Mantua, as "my fellow rooster of the red crest," and Marie de' Medici as "our most Christian, fellow queen hen" (cited in Johnson, 2011, p. 76). The impertinence was overlooked because, in effect, Martinelli was not speaking in his own person.

Madness, which could serve as a kind of disguise, allowed the actress who played an *innamorata,* in the throes of the character's distress, to appear in such disarray as to expose her breasts under the pretense that they were not the breasts of the actress that were being exposed, but of her character. The character masks, together with the fact that the performances were improvised, not written out, served to avoid censorship. The mask was not the actor and the mask, the fiction allowed, could not always be controlled. Behavior that is unacceptable, observed Castiglione in 1528, may be appropriate if the wearer "is disguised; and even if this were in such a way that everyone recognized him, it would not be a problem or possibly give offence" (Twycross and Carpenter, 2002, pp. 67–68). Meg Twycross and Sarah Carpenter reiterate, "Whether the disguise is truly impenetrable or merely symbolic, the mask seems to signal a (potentially dangerous) freedom from normal restraint between individuals" (2002, p. 71).

Put more strongly, the mask could serve to liberate the actor from his own self-censoring. The fundamental paradox of all acting, Peter Brook observes, is that "because you are in safety, you can go into danger. It is very strange, but all theatre is based on that. Because there is a greater security, you can take greater risks; and because here it is *not* you, and therefore everything about you is hidden, you can let yourself appear. The mask, in particular absolves you in that way, the fact that it gives you something to hide behind makes it unnecessary for you to hide" (Brook, 1987, p. 231). Masked acting could be great acting. It allowed the actor to recognize truth and speak it to power.

It is, more mundanely, a commonplace that the mask required the actor to rely more on physical expression than if he were not masked. Eduardo De Filippo, wearing the half-mask of Pulcinella in a 1973 video available on YouTube entitled "Eduardo De Filippo in l'arte di Pulcinello" (accessed July 25, 2019) makes abundantly clear that the face can still be highly expressive. Nonetheless, one should not underestimate the importance of speech to the commedia dell'arte in the period under consideration, when it was at its height. Verbal facility included "copiousness" in which Italian speakers still excel: variety, wit, and a tongue that is both ready and sharp (Burke, [1987] 2005, p. 80).[8] The mask forced the actor to use his voice to the greatest extent possible to convey emotions.[9] The limited facial expression required the audience to focus on speech (Wiles, 2007, pp. 128, 132).

For the actor there were other advantages to the mask. The fixity of the character mask employed by the actor allowed him to perfect the role while ostensibly improvising but actually relying more or less on memorized material, set speeches, and *lazzi* (primarily visual gags) that could be called up as suited the situation indicated by the scenario. He could comfortably inhabit the mask he generally played for life. The mask allowed the masked actor to play the role even if he was too young or too old for it. Giovanni Pellesini reportedly played the role of the servant Pedrolino into his eighty-seventh year (Lea, [1934] 1962, p. 263, note 1). By playing the same role for many years, the actor could become famous in it.

The scenarios were double or sometimes triple plotted. Despite having to play in a large number of complexly plotted scenarios, the actors were enabled by the masks to know who was who on stage at any moment. He or she could know what to anticipate in interactions with other actors similarly working within the parameters of their own mask (Wiles, 1991, p. 142). Grounded in the mask, the actor could readily adapt to new situations in new scenarios.

Utility of character masks for scenarists

The scenarist, the *capocomico* (troupe manager), knew the actors in his troupe and the characters they played; the two *vecchi*, two *zanni*, four youths, a captain, and perhaps a female servant – about ten characters in all. He knew the characters well. He might add a few characters in addition to these, particularly if he could write scenes so as to allow for role doubling, as the masks readily enabled him to do, thus keeping performance costs down.[10] He knew the characters' clothing, including hats, and the attributes of the characters, the swords of the young men and the captain, and Pantalone's money pouch, and he and the actors knew how to make use of them. For the comedies, he knew the range of the kinds of interactions in which the characters routinely engaged: the fathers futilely lusted after young women, raged against the servants for their laziness and deceit, and chastised sons and daughters, who regularly fell in love with people not of his choosing. And he knew the strengths and weaknesses of the actors playing the roles. He knew what *lazzi* they played and what speeches they knew. So he could begin with these things in mind as he was devising the world's first sitcoms.

To some extent, he could count on the audiences' familiarity with the characters and their expectations for them. This familiarity allowed the scenarist to focus on action rather than exposition, particularly if there was a prologue. The repeated use of the same masks provided the way to borrow from earlier scenarios with their similar characters. The scenarist could generate scenarios with greater rapidity than if he were writing an original play with new characters. Thus, he could provide a considerable variety of scenarios for a sponsoring duke to choose from or for a lengthy stay somewhere. And he could count on the actor knowing, in general, how to respond to and enhance the situation he had created, and on his or her knowing the kind of dialogue to provide.

The masks allowed the scenarist as well as the actor to explore situations too sensitive to explore without them: class relationships, sexuality out of bounds, hostility toward the foreign occupier, violence.

Utility of character masks for the commedia dell'arte troupe in general

When an actor leaves a television series, writers may need to kill off the character. When a commedia troupe member left – and there appears to have been considerable movement between troupes – the fixed role could be taken by another actor experienced in it. The scenarist might adapt the scenario to the particular strengths and weaknesses of the new actor but the character could live on with the performances of the troupe relatively undisturbed.

The repeated use of the same masks and their attendant costumes along with the fixed street setting and few props required for comedy allowed the troupes to function very economically and to move from city to city with limited baggage.

In a busy piazza, commedia dell'arte actors could announce themselves and the kind of performance they were about to provide by means of their identifiable masks and costumes. They could stand out from jugglers, acrobats, contortionists, rope dancers, and musicians, all of whom might be competing for attention in the piazza, some of them, like the commedia dell'arte performers on raised stages.[11] Even during Carnival, when revelers in the street were masked, the commedia performers would have been distinct because of their identifiable characters. And, as Antonio Fava (2007, p. 33) observes, "the mask is launched toward the audience." Something of the mystique of the supernatural inheres in it. And this would have attracted the audience.

Utility of character masks for the audience

The masks allowed the audience to keep the characters straight despite limited exposition and numerous and rapidly changing scenes. Their familiarity with the characters from having seen prior scenarios, if they had done so, enhanced their anticipation of what was to come.

The chief benefit for the audience and the primary reason for the widespread success of the commedia dell'arte, however, was in the distance from and perspective on daily life the performances afforded its audience. Like the masks of carnival, the masks of commedia dell'arte served to provide for and excuse temporary liberation from hierarchical relationships, privileges, rules, and taboos. But they did more than that: Flaminio Scala made explicit that he wanted his scenarios to provide "good imitation and verisimilitude."[12] And so they did. The comic scenarios, with few exceptions, represented the comic set described by the Roman Vitruvius (c. 90–c. 20 BCE) and propagated in the Renaissance by Sebastiano Serlio's drawings made in 1545: "private buildings and galleries, with windows similar to those in ordinary dwellings" (Vitruvious, 1826, p. 145). The scene showed the people and life one might find in any early modern Italian or, for that matter, any European city. The distance provided by the masks, the stage, and the framing scenario allowed the audience to see the tensions in their everyday relationships within their cultural context and, for the length of the performance at least, to gain a perspective on them that allowed it to laugh at them, and even to imagine a different life. Women freely performing in theatre in the strongly patriarchal society, and the independent characters they increasingly played, must have provided a considerable release and even inspiration for the females in the audience.

In real life, hunger plagued the streets. Peasants poured into the cities in search of employment. The poor were everywhere, some surviving as beggars, hustlers, and swindlers of every kind. Even among those lucky enough to be employed as servants, ill-treatment, job insecurity, and hunger were common. Masters, rightly or not, deplored their servants' stupidity or feared the possibility of their disloyalty, dishonesty, and thievery.

The children of citizens chafed beneath the control of their fathers. An upper-class young man was financially under the control of his father who arranged a marriage for him and negotiated a suitable dowry. Often, he did not marry until he was in his thirties, at which time he was still regarded as a youth.[13] Only when married did he become a citizen. Aimless, meanwhile, or sent to college or, even then, the son might occupy himself with whoring and street fighting. The father reasonably feared loss of control over the son and, with that, loss of the most important thing in his life, namely honor. The daughter was kept sheltered in the house doing handiwork. Only rarely was she taught to read. Reading *novelle* might lead to foolish ideas. She might take to the streets, meet young irresponsible youths, lose her chastity, and with that her marriage prospects, and her father's and the family's honor. With that fear in mind, the father married his daughter off as soon as possible, as a young adolescent, to a man usually considerably older than she.

Because servitude could begin at the age of 7 or 8, some offspring and servants had grown up together, both oppressed by the father/head-of-household. The father might reasonably fear betrayal by offspring and servants in collusion. Any threat to patriarchal control was by extension a threat to the very structure of the state.

In the scenarios, we see hungry and beleaguered servants indulging in food fantasies or in deviously obtained food. We see them outwitting and humiliating their masters, often in the aid of the masters' children, or merely to get even, or to humiliate the old men. We see young men moving out from the control of their fathers, sometimes stealing from them with the aid of a servant in order to do so, and marrying young women of their choosing. We see young women in the streets, even leaving town in disguise as gypsies, pilgrims, and, more daringly, as young men, resourcefully eluding arranged marriages with considerably older men and marrying the men they love. Stephen Orgel (1996, p. 74) observes that "plays about love matches" as commedia dell'arte scenarios almost always were, "are especially powerful fantasies of freedom in a patriarchal society, for women even more than for men. The scenarios, in endless exaggerated variations, examine the fears of the fathers and masters and the fantasies of the children.

In real life, the rising middle class – merchants and professional men – threatened not only their inferiors but also the existence of the aristocracy. In the scenarios, we see the old men, representatives of this middle class, as avaricious and lustful, in pursuit of women, as ill-befits their dignity, and endlessly gullible, slow to recognize the tricks their servants and children play on them. The professional man is given to macaronic speechifying rather than to words of wisdom. The real threat to the aristocracy from the rising middle class of merchants and professionals is belittled. And in the end no serious harm appears to have been done to the hierarchy. It remains intact. The resolution in the comedies is always an (improbably) happy one. At the same time, in the process of getting to it, the strict hierarchical control and its resulting abuses are challenged.

The Captain was a character that had particular resonance in Italy where he stood in for a *condottiero* or as a Spanish captain. A *condottiero* was a leader of a band of mercenaries hired by a ducal state, sometimes a landless Italian nobleman. Such men were too often scoundrels, ready to change sides, loathe to fight, and all too willing to settle all with a bribe. Some became rich and powerful. Others, when not employed, might wander the streets. By the time of the commedia dell'arte, the ceremonial combat of the *condottieri* with their breastplates and swords had become obsolete. Their medieval equipment was replaced by firearms and gunpowder. The story of their infamy lived on. Alternatively, the Captain could be a stand-in for the Spanish, many parts of Italy of which Spain controlled. Resentment of that control and of the disorderly conduct and rapacity of Spanish captains in Italy was expressed in the commedia dell'arte through the representation of the mask of the Spanish Captain, a fop, a coward, and a braggart, usually vainly in search of a woman. The ridiculous mask provided mockery of both.

Noted historian Peter Burke ([1987] 2005, p. 23) sees the masks as good sources for social history; they reveal "a good deal of the concerns and values of the culture in reality"; they reveal "how contemporaries perceived one another (or at least how some groups perceived others)."

The masks, because of their familiarity to scenarists and actors, along with the prodigious amount of material the actors had memorized and could employ with endless variations as needed, allowed the actors to improvise. And this improvisation, like a sporting event, provided the special excitement of a one-time-only event performed for the benefit of the audience at hand. It might fail, especially given the complex intrigue of the comedy. The non-illusory convention of the masks along with other non-illusory conventions of the commedia dell'arte, like disguises and tricks piled on tricks, promised the excitement that not only the intrigue might fail but the actors along with it. In addition, the comedies of the commedia dell'arte, greatly enhanced or permitted by the masks, allowed fantasies of a better life or at least of revenge and these too were exciting.

The city and comic masks

Renaissance comedy was city comedy and represented urban life and the tensions within it. The set for the comedy in the collections under consideration almost always accords with the description provided by Vitruvius. That fixed single city setting is consistent with both the neoclassic requirements for unity of place and for verisimilitude. Scala used it for all but one of his forty comic scenarios. The exception, Day 6, *Il vecchio geloso*, is set before a similarly fixed and verisimilar country house. Scala believed that comedies should provide a "mirror of human life."[14] His comedies include only the characters that one might meet on a city street or, in the one case, Day 6, on the road in front of Pantalone's country house. In the main, the scenarios included in the Corsini and Locatelli collections similarly abide by neoclassical guidelines: most of the Corsini comedies, for instance, are set only on the single city street or piazza and contain no characters one might not realistically meet there. The best-known masks are from the comedies and their city streets and piazzas.

Character masks in other than comedy

The same character masks, the old men, the *zanni*, the lovers, the captain can appear in all the genres. Elsebeth Aasted counted Pantalone's appearance in ninety-six of the 100 Corsini scenarios (Aasted, 1992, p. 165). But given the themes of tragedy, tragicomedy, and pastoral scenarios, different from those of comedy, it is no surprise that the character masks we identify with the comedies are even more wide-ranging in their professions than in the comedies. For instance, Pantalone, whom we know best in the comedies as a Venetian merchant, appears in other forms, variously as a doctor, a governor, a secretary, an innkeeper, a tutor, a magician, an envoy of the king, or as a counselor to him.

Neapolitan commedia dell'arte theorist Andrea Perrucci, acknowledging in 1699 that the character masks familiar from comedy (where they were a "necessity") appeared in both tragedies and tragicomedies – and, I add, pastorals – begged that unless the roles were comic, their actors "should not perform using masks but make use of their own faces" (Perrucci, [1699] 2008, pp. 21–22). While it is true that the prop lists do not mention masks for the familiar characters appearing in genres other than comedy, any more than they do in the comedies themselves, it seems likely that the actors identified by their familiar mask names would, in fact, have played the roles masked and with their characteristic dialect and movement, regardless of the profession of the character. Otherwise there would have been no point in identifying them by their names and the audience would have found it more difficult to keep the characters in the complex plots straight, particularly if they were familiar with the comedies, in which they were masked. Mengarelli points out that the crude watercolors in the Corsini collection are highly schematic: Coviello is a servant in Corsini I/13, "*Il mago*" and a patriarch in Corsini I/26, "*La pellagrina*," but that he is nonetheless shown in the same costume in both watercolors (Mengarelli, 2014, p. 137). Pantalone, always in red and in slippers, can be readily identified as Pantalone, etc. I take these schematic representations as evidence that it was important to identify the character masks as such and that it was important to play the roles with masks.

Robert Henke comments that there are so few tragedies in the period because "in the absolutist climate of northern Italian courts, it was much easier to represent bourgeois, urban vices than to stage the evils of political tyrants." On this account, he argues, "renaissance tragedies remained a more strictly academic genre" (Henke, 1997, p. 19). The two commedia dell'arte tragedies available in print, of the total of four in the three collections I consider, are safely set in foreign lands. Their city setting grander and more ambitious than that of the comedies, similarly conform to neoclassical requirements.[15] The masks we know from comedy may, but need not, appear but generally in more dignified roles. The more elaborate set requirements and the costumes for the royalty, who were the subjects of tragedy, would also have been very expensive. Andrew Gurr reports that in Shakespeare's England "The Earl of Leicester paid £543 for seven doublets and two cloaks, at an average cost for each item rather higher than the price Shakespeare paid for a house in Stratford" (Gurr, 1980, p. 13). The aristocrats would probably not have been masked, masks having more to do, in the first instance, with comic or frightening characters or shadows. They could have been identified by their elegant and expensive clothing including headwear and by their bearing, and attributes. There were strict sumptuary laws, laws controlling expenditures or extravagance in clothing. Stephen Orgel remarks that the wardrobe of Henslowe's company, the Lord Chamberlain's Men, included " 'a robe for to go invisible' asserting in a culturally specific manner how perfectly garments determined the way one was to be seen, and not seen" (Orgel, 1996, p. 101).[16]

Scala's comic scenarios and his single tragedy are faithful to Vitruvious and to the kinds of characters that might with verisimilitude appear in their respective settings, perhaps because, intending his scenarios for print, he wanted both to impress the humanists with his knowledge of neoclassicism and avoid the opprobrium of the Church. A number of the scenarios set in the city in the Corsini and Locatelli collections are relatively freer of neoclassical constraints. For one thing, in them, the city could serve, not only for the few tragedies and for the comedies, but also for tragicomedies, a genre in itself, according to the Renaissance moral philosopher, Giason de Nores, who railed against it shortly before his death in 1590, as "a monstrous and irregular composition" mixing the high tone of tragedy with the low tone of comedy (Sidnell, 1991, p. 48).

Other masks

In turning my attention to other masks, I consider several different kinds of figures, one cannot really call them characters, some of which are masked and some not. The most interesting of these are found in the pastoral settings, sometimes specified as Arcadia or the forest. In the Corsini and Locatelli collections, but not in the Scala, some specific kinds of figures appear in the city as well.

Some Corsini and Locatelli tragicomedies set in the city also violate verisimilitude by including personified abstractions like "Hope," "Despair," "Time," and "Love." Sometimes these figures are manifest only as offstage voices, or they appear in a prologue or epilogue but in other instances, they appear in the scenario proper. When they did appear on stage, I believe that, like such figures in Renaissance paintings, they were identified in performance by the context in which they appeared, in the case of the scenarios, a verbal context,[17] and by their costumes including headwear, and by their bearing, and attributes.[18] No masks for the personifications are listed in the prop list, whereas, as we shall see, in the pastorals, masks are specified for some other kinds of figures. An oracle is employed in a number of the tragicomedies, sometimes specified as only a voice. In three instances an oracle is mentioned in the prop lists, suggesting some kind of visual manifestation, perhaps a statue. In a few of the scenarios, a shadow appears that comes between fighting men, effectively separating them. In one scenario, Corsini I/24, "*Il giusto principe*," the prop list specifies that the shadow wears a black house coat and skirt; the shadow is evidently female. In the line drawings accompanying Giovanni Briccio's *commedia ridicolosa La Rosmira*, 1676, a fully scripted play intended to be performed by amateurs in imitation of commedia dell'arte, the shadow is draped from head to toe (Briccio, 1676, p. 11).

Scala's comic scenarios (he provides no tragicomedies) include only fake magicians. The Corsini and Locatelli city scenarios, by contrast, sometimes include what was to be understood as real magic. The magician can be identified in the Corsini watercolors by his short gown, his distinctive headdress, his rod, as in Corsini I/13, "*Il mago*" and sometimes also by a spell book, both attributes sometimes mentioned in the prop lists (Figure 3.1, p. 67).

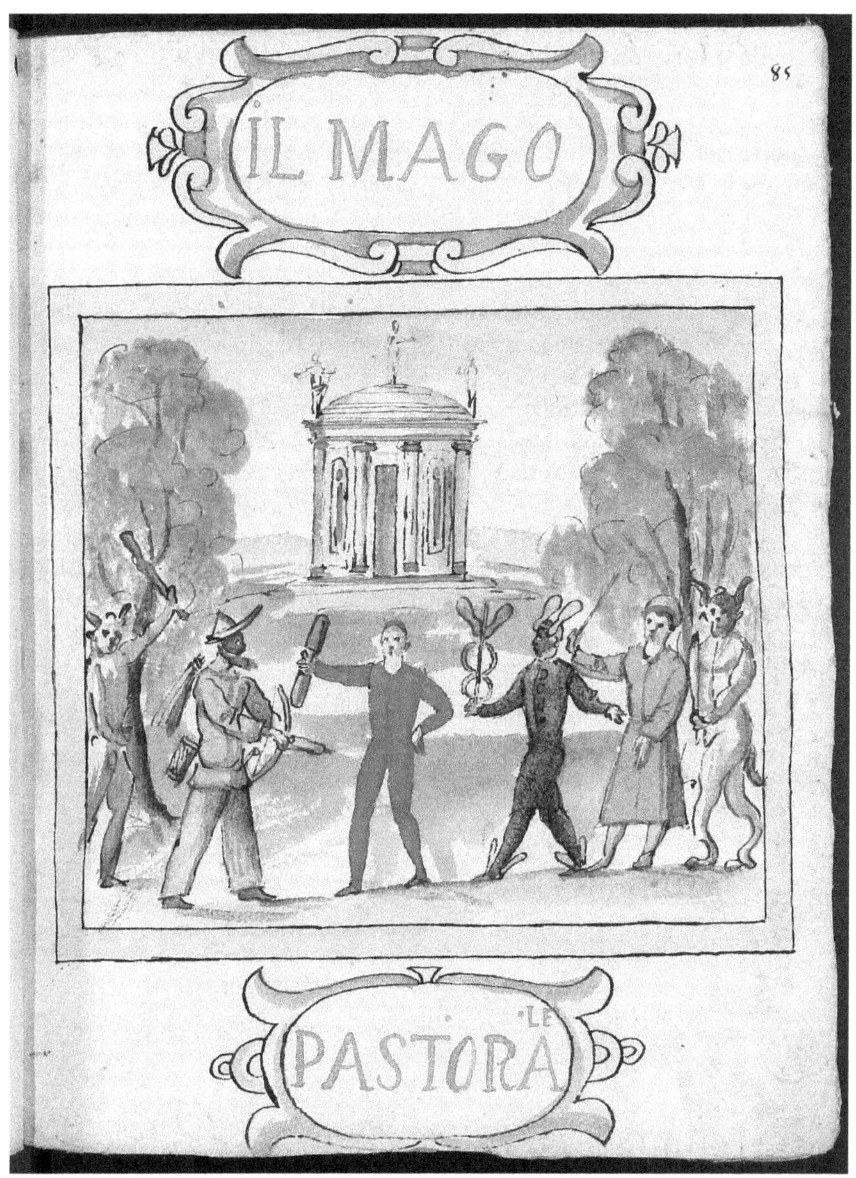

Figure 3.1 Frontispiece "*Il mago.*" (n.d.). Anonymous pen and watercolor. "*Raccolta di scenari più scelti d'istrioni divisi in due volume.*" MS 45.G. 5. (Biblioteca Corsiniana, Rome). Vol 1, number 13.

Source: By permission of the Accademia Nazionale dei Lincei e Corsiniana.

His short gown and both attributes are shown in *La Rosmira* (Figure 3.2, below. See also Briccio, 1676, pp. 7, 55, 92, and 105).

The Council of Trent, 1563, "absolutely repudiated" magic arts.[19] "To believe that anything other than God could bring about magical ends was implicitly to turn away from Him" (Ferber, 2015, p. 171). On that account, the practice of magic, whether others were harmed by it or not, could be a serious offense. It might be associated with the devil (Gentilcore, 2006, p. 313). And indeed, the magicians in the Corsini and Locatelli scenarios set in the city are sometimes accompanied by devils or other evil spirits: see for instance, Corsini, 1/43, "*La pazzia di Doralice*."

Devils and spirits are regularly masked to make them look ugly and frightening, consistent with their moral ugliness; a correlation between visual and moral ugliness having been assumed in the Renaissance. The conception of these figures came from representations of medieval demons.[20] A mask and costume for a devil in the city is specifically mentioned in Corsini I/31, "*Le moglie superbe*." Paintings from the period indicate that the devil or demons would also have been horned, with cloven hooves, and shaggy lower extremities and tails, as they are shown in the Corsini watercolor I/13, "*Il mago*," where they also bear clubs (Figure 3.1, p. 67). In the Correr scenario collection, variously dated to the first or second half of the seventeenth century, the prop list for "*La costanza di Flaminia con le furbarie di Stoppino*" specifies masks for the spirits (Alberti, 1996, p. 171).

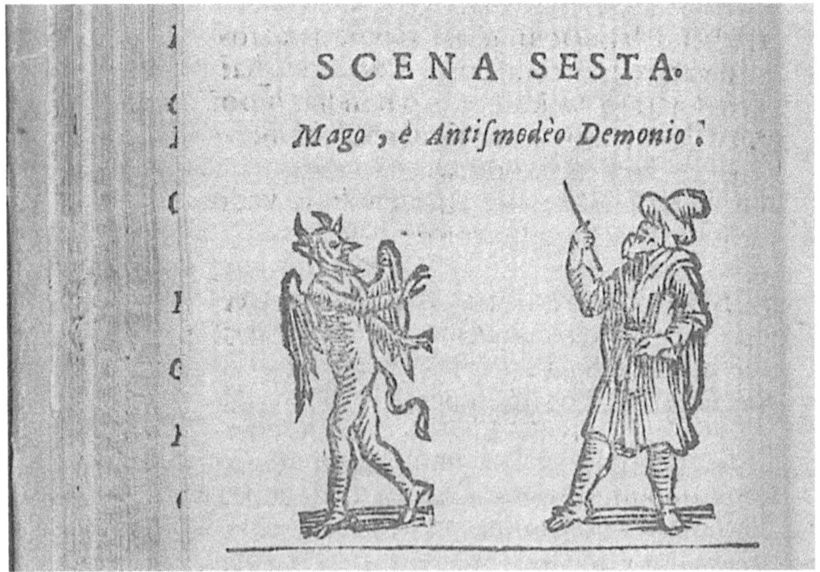

Figure 3.2 Giovanni Briccio. *La Rosmira*. Woodcut. (Rome: Biblioteca Nazionale. p. 74.

Source: By permission Biblioteca Nazionale, Rome.

While witchcraft and magic do not accord with the verisimilitude called for in the city setting, or with the teachings of the church, they were, in fact, a part of everyday life. One might consider magicians as a part of the deceit and simulation that were at the heart of baroque culture. Magic provided a livelihood and satisfied deep psychological needs. Cultural historian Guido Ruggiero observes that, "in the Renaissance, every town and village needed its witches and magicians."[21]

> Witchcraft and magic were involved in a wide range of Renaissance ways of thinking about and dealing with the everyday world. And crucially they played a central role in emphasizing the way in which that everyday world – often assumed to be materialistic, static, and limited – was closely and deeply integrated with a complex, dynamic, and powerful spiritual world.
>
> (Ruggiero, 2002, pp. 448, 881)

In the main, the magicians in the city, unlike the magicians in the forest, who employ considerably more power, do little more than set fires[22] and provide special waters effecting cures, albeit sometimes with the aid of the devil, as in Corsini I/43, "*La pazzia di Doralice.*" In most city scenarios, lacking a magician, we are asked to accept that cures for the likes of madness or feigned death were provided by a doctor with potions from an apothecary.

Some scenarios may indicate their creator's discomfort with city magic, however benign or beneficent. In Corsini, II/40, "*Il veleno,*" a comedy, the magician, a necromancer who works with the devil had been banished from the city because of his art. He resides in the forest. When he heals both Fabritio and Isabella, the ban is lifted. But his acceptance back into society and the city evidently depends upon his abjuring his art. He therefore throws his rod and book into the fire. In the comedy Locatelli, I/44, "*Il fonte incantato,*" a cure is effected by magic in the city but the magician instructs Flavio to obtain the healing water from a lion-guarded fountain in the forest. In Corsini, II/48, "*Le teste incantate,*" a tragicomedy, Pantalone seeks to prevent the death of his daughter through the aid of a magician whom he must go to the forest to fetch. The trips to the forest, while seeming to work around genre barriers and the Church's prohibition against magic by making the mythological forest its home, then fail to provide the unity of place called for by neoclassicism, despite the specification in some scenarios, like Locatelli's I/4, "*La innocentia rivenuta*" that both city and forest (probably to facilitate rapid changes between locales) were on the stage at the same time: "*Una parte di bosco in scena.*"[23] In scenarios set in the city, the forest may have been established by no more than the single prop, mentioned in the prop list for "*Le teste incantate*" and in prop lists for several other scenarios as well.

In a number of cases, the Corsini and Locatelli versions of the same story are designated as being in different genres, indicating the confusion or perhaps a measure of disregard for genre designations and their settings and the masks that might appear in them. Indeed a single scenario within the same collection may be placed in one genre on its title page and in another at its conclusion: see, for instance, Corsini, II/50, and Locatelli I/4, and I/10. And even when the text does not indicate such genre confusion, the scenario may not easily fit into the genre into which it was placed. Hulfeld observes that the Corsini comedy II/40 "*Il veleno*" has characters and figures better suited to a tragicomedy or a pastoral: a lord, a count, his courtiers, a necromancer, and devils. Its opening scene includes a blood-soiled weapon and the deposition of the dead body in the forest in the darkness of night that can hardly be reconciled with the genre of comedy (Hulfeld, 2014, p. 1262). The corresponding story in Locatelli, I/5 "*Il veneno*" is designated a tragicomedy. Other scenarios present genre problems as well: Corsini, II/44, "*La magica di Pantalone*," a comedy, is set in a city but has a mountain, and after Pantalone, the magician, unearths a fortune there, Zanni and Trappolino are dragged into the resulting hole by a dangerous ghost, and return to the city with diabolical tails that they got in that hole.

The pastoral mode

Scholars now frequently refer to pastoral as a mode, that is, as a literary method, mood, or manner, rather than as a genre.[24] The pastoral mode comfortably accommodates both comedy and tragicomedy. It also seems to make way for other experimental works, like Corsini II/4, "*Elisa alii bassà*," identified as an Opera turchesca (a Turkish work) that takes place entirely in a forest, or like Locatelli I/51, "*Li ritratti*" a pastoral pescatoria, (a fisherman's pastoral), a reworking of Locatelli 1/3 "*Li ritratti*" a pastoral tragi-comedy.

The natural home for magic seems to be the pastoral, specified in the scenarios as a forest or arcadia. It's what Louise George Clubb refers to as the "green world" or the "Arcadian Elsewhere" making clear that the pastoral is unmoored from reality (Clubb, 1989, p. 165). The magic that occurs there, initiated by the magician or otherwise, seems to have been limited only by what imagination, money, and technology could provide. The Arcadian Elsewhere could include comic masks, classical gods, humans costumed as animals, devils, nymphs, satyrs, puppets, humans transformed into animals, or into trees and flowers.

A rather ambitious, but far from unique example of a pastoral, Locatelli II/26 "*La nave*," requires a grotto from which spirits and flames can come, a temple from which Bacchus can appear, a tree, an exploding rock, fire, fireworks, the sea with a storm and from which the Captain can appear riding on a dolphin and into which a ship with characters in it can sink, a tower into which the Magician can retire, and from which he is struck by a flash and turned into a stone, the sky from which Jove speaks, clouds from which Mars speaks, lightening, and a magic fountain. It decidedly does not provide the appearance of reality and the occurrences within it are not verisimilar.

While some of the pastorals may have been staged very simply, and indeed M.A. Katritzky finds definitive evidence that full-length pastorals of a commedia dell'arte type were performed by mountebanks in 1598 on a raised platform with no backdrop and minimal props (Katritzky, 1998, p. 119), scenarios in pastoral settings were conducive to elaborate spectacle and these settings were scenario specific. Such spectacles could only have been paid for by dukes, to be shown in their private theatres, likely for a one-time-only performance before an invited audience. The cast for a pastoral might be large, the set construction expensive and requiring numerous stagehands to maneuver. For the Medici wedding of 1589, a cloud bearing a human, like those specified in a number of the pastoral scenarios, required a crew of ten to twelve men to operate (Saslow, 1996, p. 85). The most successful commedia dell'arte companies were able to rent theatres for public performances but the costs involved in the production of many of the pastorals would likely have meant that they would not often have chosen to play them before a general audience. And while the elaborate theatricalism of many pastorals would have held appeal for a general audience, its interior world of emotion, particularly that of courtly love and its attendant lengthy laments and persuasions in verse, the style of which we have direct evidence of from codas to some of the pastorals, would seem to have been intended primarily for a niche audience.[25] Because professional troupes of commedia dell'arte players performed both regular scripted pastoral plays in addition to the improvised ones, they would have been very familiar with the language involved.

The comedies' themes of old men lusting after young girls and invariably getting tricked and humiliated in the pursuit, of youths, by hook or by crook, getting to marry those of their own choosing, of servants outwitting their masters, and of the exposure of the braggart captain as a coward were, to judge by the relative number of pastoral and comic scenarios, far more popular. And as the iconography shows, comedies, at least the majority of the comedies, uncomplicated by forests, the sea, and gods in the heavens, or by tragedy with its attendant palaces, could be readily played on a raised stage in the street with curtain openings for windows and doors, the same portable set representing any city.[26] It is the comedies and their character masks that everyone knew.

Pastoral masks

Devils and spirits appear in the pastoral setting as well as in the city. There are, however, quite a number of kinds of figures that are unique to the pastoral setting: there are the shepherds, nymphs, satyrs and wildmen as one might expect, but there are also classical gods, and, in addition to actual animals also present in a few of the comedies, humans representing animals along with sea creatures represented by puppets, and humans magically transformed into animals.

Shepherds, nymphs, satyrs, and wildmen

We have numerous verbal and visual records of how, at least for the fully scripted drama, the shepherds and nymphs likely looked on stage. Playwright and director Leone de'Sommi, in 1556, in Lisa Sampson's paraphrase,

> recommends that a shepherd should wear a light silk, sleeveless undershirt . . . covered in front and behind by animal skins, and that his arms

> and legs could be bare if he was young and good-looking, or covered with a skin-coloured body stocking if not. He could wear a wig and a crown of ivy or laurel, and his props might include a small flask or decorated wooden bowl tied to his belt, a knapsack, or a staff – and the more "extravagant" this was the better. The nymphs, who [in the scripted drama unlike in commedia dell'arte] were usually played by boys required a fairly elaborate, long-sleeved tunic, covered by a brightly coloured skirt fastened by a gold or coloured belt, and a rich cloak over one shoulder. Their thick blond hair (probably a wig) could be covered by a veil and worn loose, as long as it appeared natural. Their costume was completed by a bow and quiver and a single spear, thus emphasizing the strong mythologizing classicizing flavour of courtly pastoral.
>
> (Sampson, 2006b, p. 179)

As evidence Sampson provides a number of representations of nymphs and shepherds from published scripted pastorals of the period, some with staffs rather than spears. Of these, I include the engraving for the frontispiece for the 1602 edition of Battista Guarini's, tragicomedy pastoral, the very influential *Il pastor fido*, originally published in 1590, in which a nymph and a shepherd are represented left and right center of the image (Figure 3.3, p. 73).

Sampson (2006b) includes a number of very similar pictures of nymphs and shepherds from several pastoral plays of the period. *La Rosmira* (Briccio, 1676) contains numerous representations of shepherds and nymphs very similar to these but in simpler and more economical attire.

The watercolor for the Corsini I/9, "*Li tre satiri*" shows two shepherds, also more practically dressed and with staffs rather than spears, but similarly crowned with leaves (Figure 3.4, p. 74).

Scala's Day 44, an heroic drama, "Rosalba incantrice" requires "four fine dresses for Nymphs," indicating a production to be paid for by the aristocracy.

According to Torquato Tasso the author of *Aminta*, 1573, which was, along with Battista Guarini's *Il pastor fido*, 1590, one of the two most famous pastoral plays ever written, satyrs should be represented as "half man, half goat, and all beast" (Perrucci, [1699] 2008, p. 23). In the engraving for the 1602 edition of *Il pastor fido* (Figure 3.3, p. 73) one can see a representation of a satyr at bottom right. And similarly, in the watercolor for Corsini I/9 "Li tre satiri" (Figure 3.4, p. 74), the three satyrs threatening the bound Pantalone with knotted clubs have cloven hooves, animal flanks, and human faces with beards, small ears and curling horns. Except for the horns, their top half is human.

A wildman is shown in the watercolor for Corsini I/45, "*Il Proteo*" (Figure 3.5, p. 75).[27] He has small animal ears and a long beard. He appears to be masked. His body is very hairy but he has human arms and legs. He holds a large club. In the frequent representations of the wildman in Renaissance art, the body hair is shown on an actual body rather than by what appears to be rendered in the Corsini as an item of clothing.

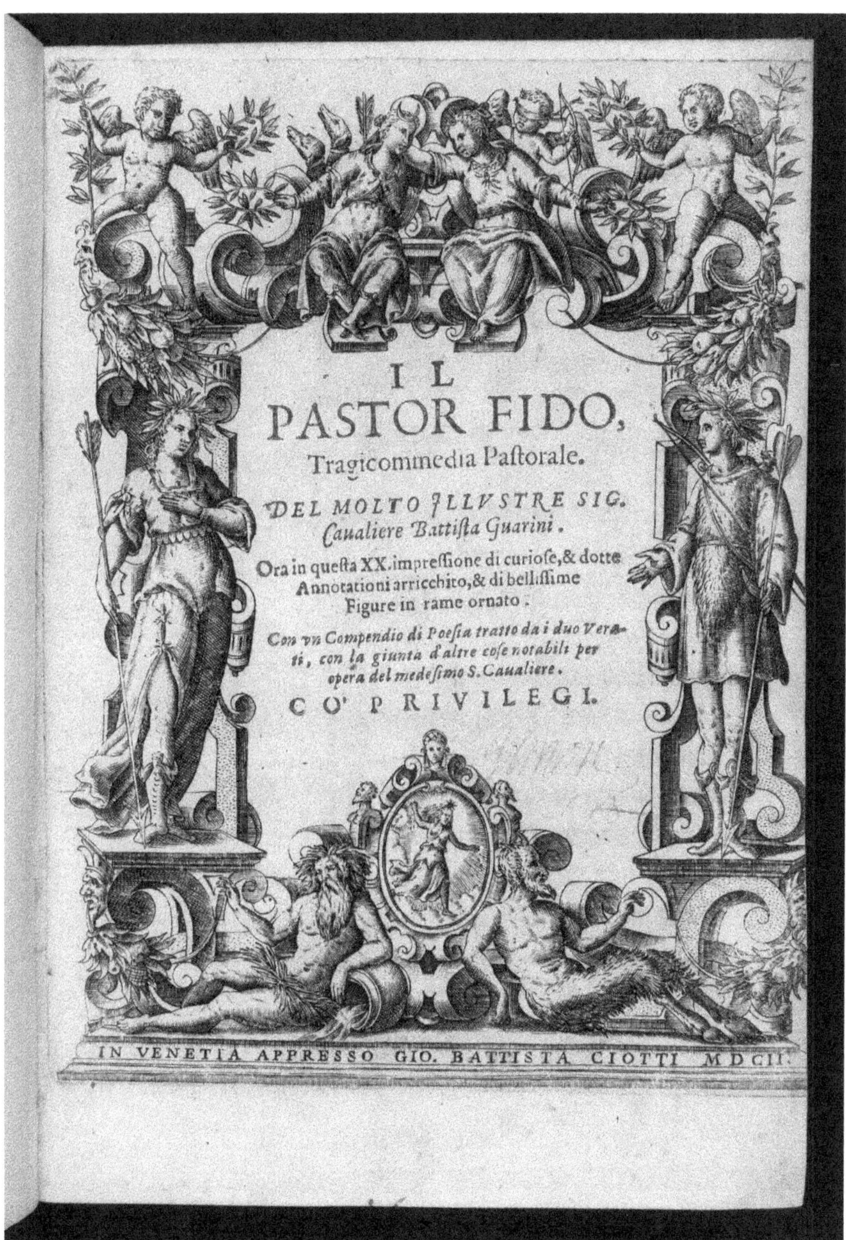
IL
PASTOR FIDO,
Tragicommedia Paſtorale.
DEL MOLTO ILLVSTRE SIG.
Caualiere Battiſta Guarini.
Ora in queſta XX. impreſſione di curioſe, & dotte
Annotationi arricchito, & di belliſſime
Figure in rame ornato.
Con vn Compendio di Poeſia tratto da i duo Verati, con la giunta d'altre coſe notabili per
opera del medeſimo S. Caualiere.
CO' PRIVILEGI.
IN VENETIA APPRESSO GIO. BATTISTA CIOTTI MDCII.

Figure 3.3 Francesco Val (l)egio? (1602). Engraved frontispiece for Battista Guarini's *Il pastor fido*. (Reading: Reading University Library). Overstone Shelf 19F/19).

Source: By permission of Reading University Library.

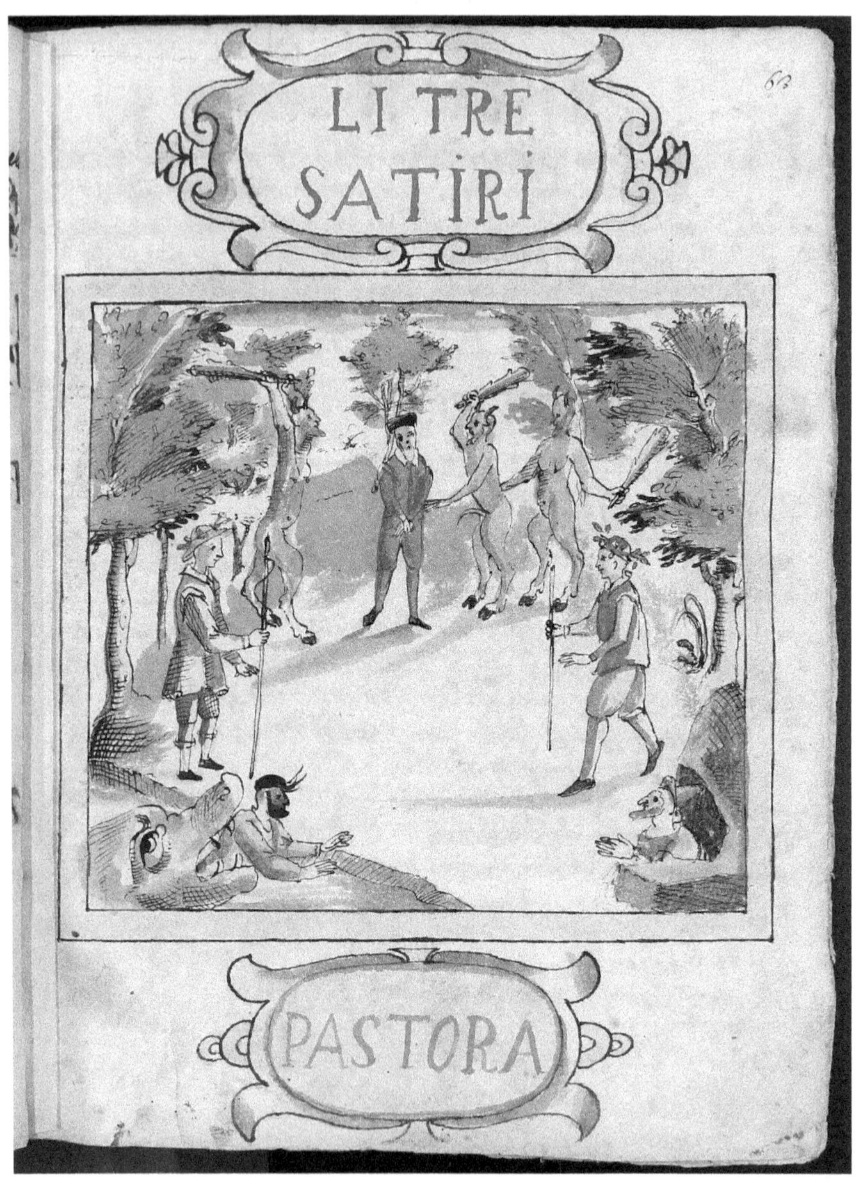

Figure 3.4 Frontispiece "*Li tre satiri.*" (n.d.). Anonymous pen and watercolor. "*Raccolta di scenari più scelti d'istrioni divisi in due volume.*" MS 45.G. 5. (Biblioteca Corsiniana, Rome). Vol. 1, number 9.

Source: By permission of the Accademia Nazionale dei Lincei e Corsiniana.

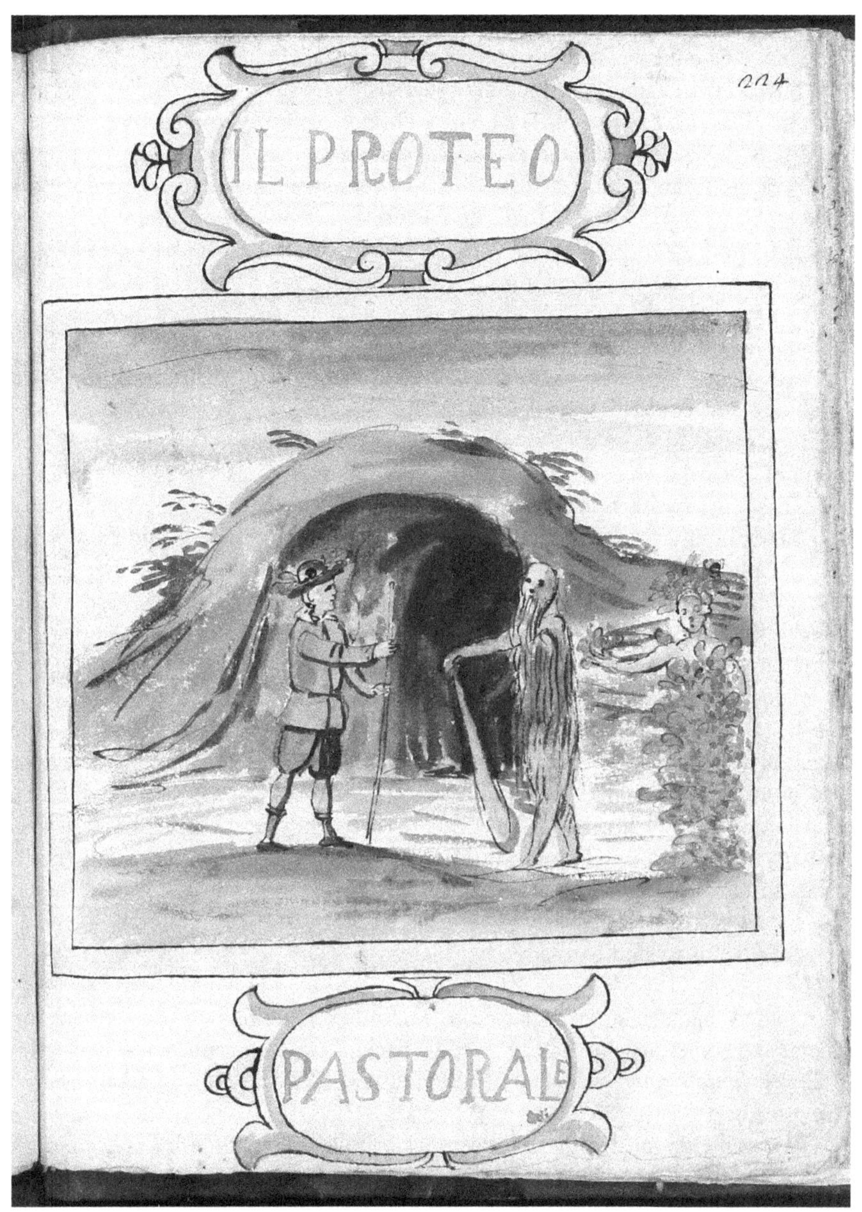

Figure 3.5 Frontispiece "*Il Proteo.*" (n.d.). Anonymous pen and watercolor. "*Raccolta di scenari più scelti d'istrioni divisi in due volume.*" MS 45.G. 5. (Biblioteca Corsiniana, Rome). Vol. 1, number 45.

Source: By permission of the Accademia Nazionale dei Lincei e Corsiniana.

Classical gods

Gods (with the exception of the Goddess of Peace, who appears as a *deus ex machina* in Corsini II/32) do not appear in the city. Their appearances in the pastorals, however, are numerous: including that of Jove, Pluto, Venus, Mars, Mercury, Bacchus, Proteus, and Cupid. The many paintings of Greco-Roman myths by Italian artists in the fifteenth and sixteenth centuries, art historian Luba Freedman observes, are testament to "the fascination of humanistically educated readers [the aristocrats, who would have seen the pastorals] . . . with the cultural legacy of classical antiquity." "Familiarity with the body of well-known and lesser-known myths . . . served to indicate a person's education, and hence, social standing." (Freedman, 2011, pp. 1, 24). So the scenarios with classical gods in them complimented their audience.

These gods, the paintings suggest, were to be identified primarily by their attributes and context. In the prop list for Locatelli II/28 "*Li tre satiri,*" and in more detail in Corsini's version of the same scenario with the same title (Corsini 1/9), the character masks disguise themselves as Greek gods: Pantalone, as Zeus, by carrying a pestle for a thunder-bolt; Zanni, as Mercury, by two shoes bound to his head and two to his ankles for wings, and carrying a spit wreathed with sausage representing a caduceus. Sardinello, another Zanni, as Cupid, has shoes for wings and a half-hoop of sausage-meat for his bow. In Corsini's I/13 "*Il mago*" (Figure 3.1, p. 67), the same disguises are employed. Pantalone is Zeus, but Bertolino, a Frenchman, plays Mercury. As the Frenchman, he is clearly masked, as is the servant, Coviello, who plays Cupid (Figure 3.1, p. 67). In Elsbeth Aasted's description of the painting, Coviello has a sausage for an arrow, bundles of brushwood for wings and a boot for a quiver. Aasted also points to Pantalone's imperial hand on his hip and to Mercury's light step (Aasted, 1992, p. 178). Even if, as Stephen Orgel argues, visual imagery was verbally explicated, the humor in these examples depends upon the audience's being so familiar with the attributes and manner of the gods being represented that they were able to identify them even in the far-fetched comic representations of them provided by the readily identifiable character masks (Orgel, 2014, p. 460).

In other representations, Zeus can be further identified by his crown and shield, and sometimes by the eagle on the back of which he appears as in Corsini II/20 "*Il Pantaloncino di. v. atti*" where he is called by his Roman name, "Jove" (Figure 3.6, p. 77).

The same Corsini illustration also shows Pluto identifiable by his pitchfork and by the dragon-shaped hell-mouth with flames to his left. Note that both Jove and Pluto are nude, as gods often are in Renaissance paintings. In the frontispiece for the 1602 edition of Battista Guarini's tragicomedy pastoral, *Il pastor fido*, however, Diana and Venus, at top center, are discretely draped. Alpheus, the river god at bottom left is also discretely covered by what is perhaps seaweed. His left arm rests on an attribute, the vessel from which he pours the river (Figure 3.3, p. 73).

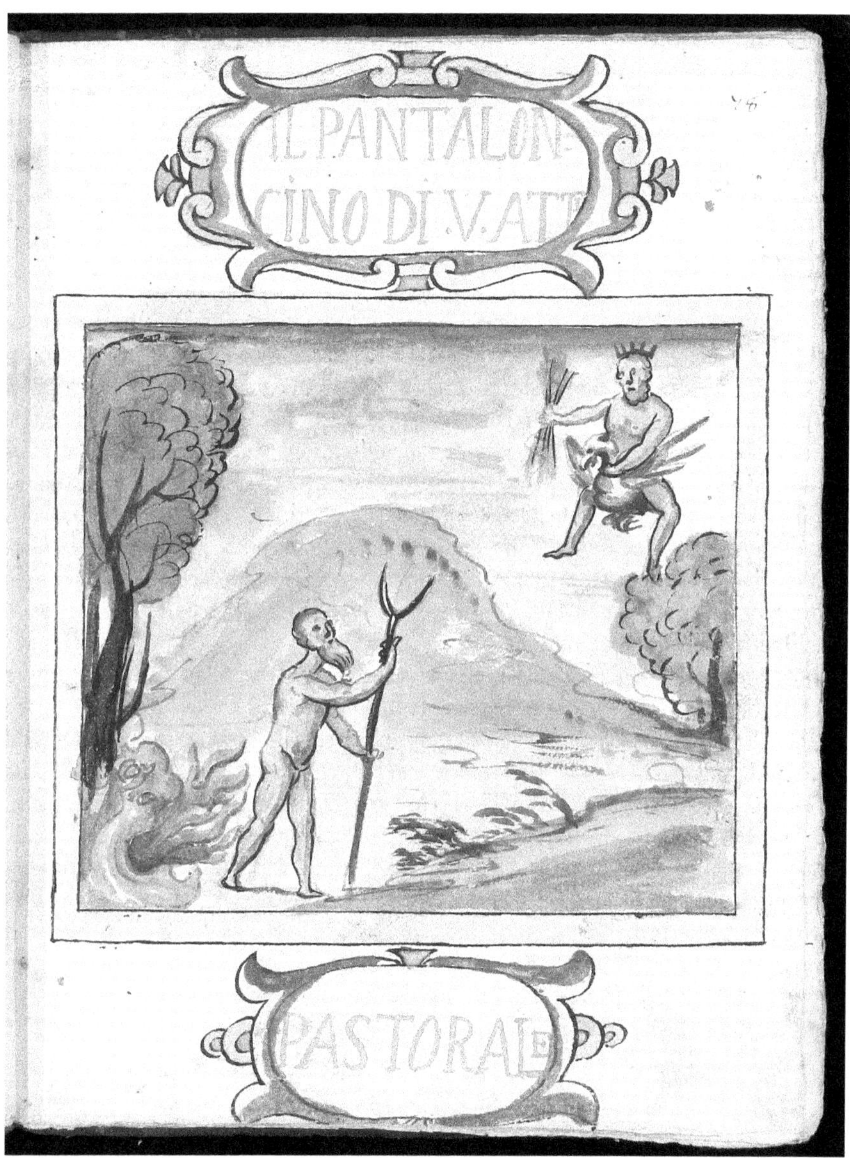

Figure 3.6 Frontispiece "*Il Pantalone di v. atti*" (n.d.). Anonymous pen and watercolor. "*Raccolta di scenari più scelti d'istrioni divisi in due volume*." MS 45.G. 6. (Biblioteca Corsiniana, Rome). Vol. I1, number 20.

Source: By permission of the Accademia Nazionale dei Corsiniana.

Real animals

Scala introduces a pack of hunting hounds into his Day 6, "*Il vecchio geloso*," a comedy, and into Day 37, "*La caccia*," also a comedy, he introduces ridiculous hunting animals: a cockerel, a monkey, and a she-cat, all live, as well as hares and other dead animals as bounty from the hunt. As we might expect in Arcadia, there are also animals: a few of them are actual: dogs, cats, and donkeys. In Corsini I/1 "*La gran pazzia di Orlando*," the real horse, Baiardo appears. In Locatelli II/1 "*Orlando furioso*," the hippogriff is specified in the cast list as a "winged horse."

Animals played by humans

Many animals in the pastorals are played by humans masked and fully costumed. The prop lists specify costumes and masks for bears, lions, and oxen. The only lions in Italy were in seraglios, that is zoos, belonging to the likes of the Medici of Florence, the Grand Duke of Tuscany and Pope Leo X (Baratay and Hardouin-Fugier, 2002, p. 19). Jacob Burckhardt states that lions sometimes served as executioners of political judgments, keeping "alive a certain terror in the popular mind" (Burckhardt, 1904, p. 293). Elizabeth Cohen and Thomas Cohen claim that there were still bears enough in Italy to provide for an occasional bearbaiting (Cohen and Cohen, 2001, p. 288). Lions appear in the *Bucolics* of Virgil, and lions and bears, both appear in Ovid's *Metamorphoses*, the latter of which, at least, heavily influenced the commedia dell'arte.

Most often in the scenarios, lions and bears played by fully costumed actors were terrifying to the character masks, as in Locatelli's I/41, "*Il Proteo*," where the lion frightens people and consequently they are delighted at its slaughter. But bears and lions could also be very gentle and solicitous. In Corsini's II/28 "*Il fonte incantato*," the lion guarding the well caresses Flavia. In Scala's Day 43, "*Alvida*," a "Royal Drama," a small boy rides a she-bear and leads a lioness on a leash. Later these animals lie down and each nurses a human baby on its teats. To protect the babies each picks one up in her jaws and carries it to safety. Animals with jaws that can carry babies seem to have been envisioned as some cross between humans dressed as an animal and puppets. Corsini I/9 "*Li tre satiri*" shows prop/puppet dolphins and whales of a size sufficient to allow them to open their jaws to expel humans (Figure 3.4, p. 74).

Harmonious animal representations: real, puppet, human

Live animals, prop/puppet animals, humans as animals and, as we shall see, humans magically transformed into animals could appear on stage in the same scenario with no sense of dissonance. Scala's Day 43, "*Alvida*" has a real donkey and a fully costumed lion and bear. In Locatelli II/50 "*Il Pantaloncino*," Jove appears astride a prop eagle, Pantalone, transformed into an ass, and a fully costumed actor meant to represent a real lion appears at the magician's behest to terrify the evil-doers. There is no evidence of any sense of discordance in the various means of representation. Together, they enlivened the spectacle.

Women transformed into trees; men transformed into animals

The most interesting and most significant of the masks, after the character masks, are masks and props used for human transformations. Ovid's *Metamorphoses* and both medieval and renaissance art, secular and religious, are full of representations of transformations and of the transformed, but clearly human, beings. Perhaps the best known of such representations is Gian Lorenzo Bernini's *Apollo and Daphne*, 1625, in which Daphne, to escape the advances of Apollo, as in Ovid's *Metamorphoses*, calls to her father the Greek river god Peneus to save her. To do so, he transforms her into a laurel tree (Figure 3.7, p. 80).

On occasion, women in the pastoral scenario, in self-defense, transform themselves. But for the most part humans in the scenarios are transformed by the magician, primarily as a means of punishment as in Florentian Antonio Tempesta's, 1606 *Circe changing Ulysses Men to Swine* (Figure 3.8, p. 81).

Rarely, humans are transformed into a stone, a flower, a fountain and, in at least one instance, into a female.

In Corsini II/16, "*Il Pantaloncino*," Ricciolina is transformed into an apple tree as punishment for her adultery that, if that were not bad enough in itself, resulted in her pregnancy. Hulfeld observes the age-old significance of the identification of the apple tree with the sinning biblical Eve (Hulfeld, 2014, p. 1025). The woman is most commonly transformed into a bay laurel tree, referred to in Psalm 37 as a tree of evil, but some women in the scenarios show themselves capable of transforming themselves into laurel trees in self-defense. So the connotation of the laurel tree is not always that of evil. Women as trees seem for the most part long-suffering: they never speak, although Olivetta in Locatelli II/50 "*Il Pantaloncino*," does manage to shriek. (Zanni recognizes the shriek as that of his wife and embraces and kisses the tree.)

Although women are usually transformed into trees, men are transformed into animals: oxen, bears, lions, mules, donkeys, even into a frog. In Corsini, I/9 "*Li tre satiri*," Franceschina is turned into a cow. While animals represented by humans appear in the cast lists as the animals they represent, humans who are transformed appear in the cast list, not as the trees or animals into which they are transformed, but as their character masks: Pantalone, Graziano, Burattino, Coviello, and Franceschina. It is the comic masks who undergo transformations into animals. Whereas an actor is fully disguised as an animal by both costume and mask, the character transformed into an animal, to deduce from the prop list, is represented as transformed almost always only by the substitution of the head of the animal for his own, and only rarely, also by the addition of a pelt as in Locatelli II/50 "*Il Pantaloncino*," where such a pelt for Pantalone is specified in the prop list. In this scenario, Burattino enters leading Pantalone, probably on all fours, transformed into an ass. Burattino remarks, "Poor old master, who would have said that you would become an ass?" Hulfeld observes that the transformation into an ass is based on the *Metamorphoses of Apuleius* as well as on Lukian's *Asinus* and is associated with shame and mockery (Hulfeld, 2014, p. 1025). Taking advantage of the transformation, the servant, with various tomfoolery, mounts the ass.

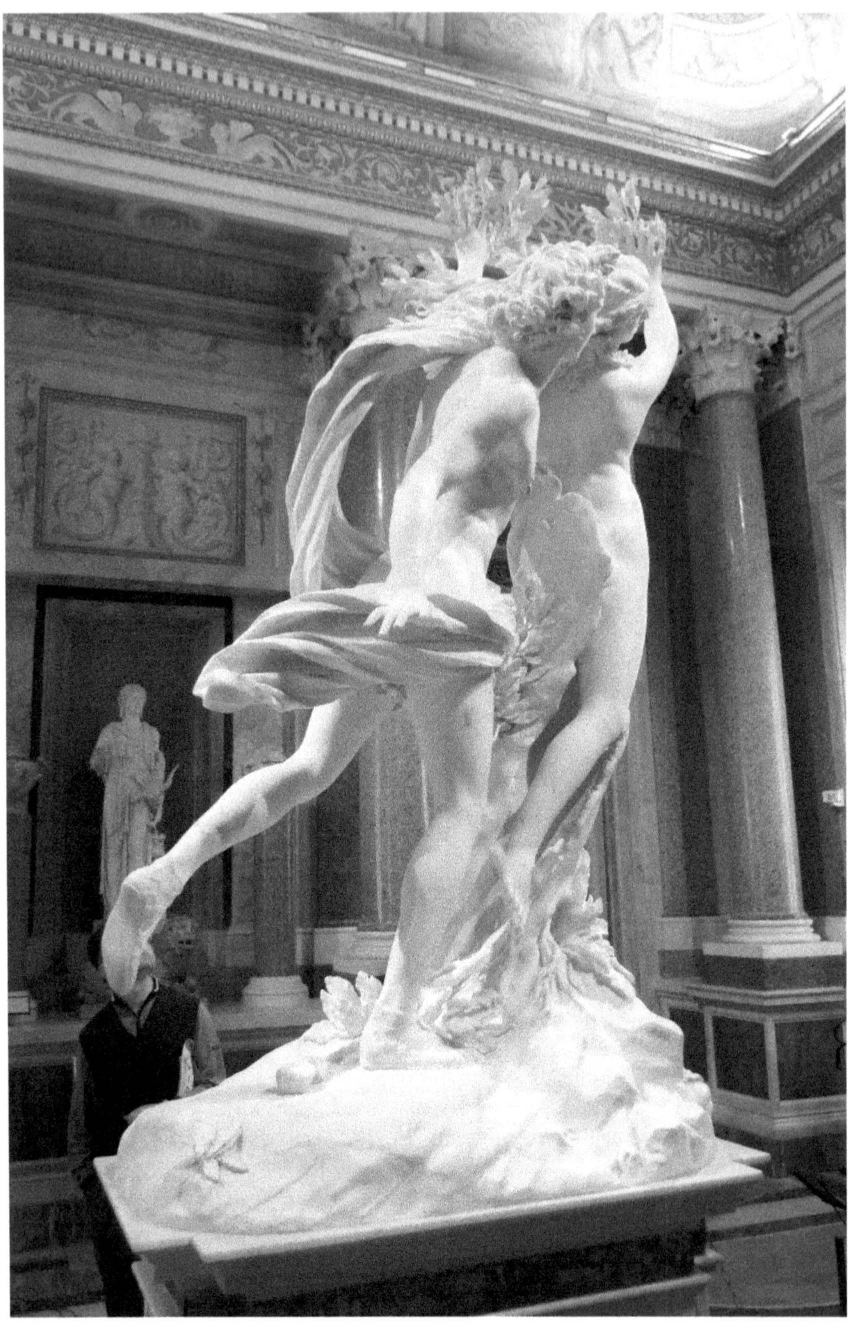

Figure 3.7 Gian Lorenzo Bernini. (c. 1625). Marble sculpture. *Apollo and Daphne*. (Galleria Borhese, Rome).

Source: Creative Commons Attribution-Share Alike 3.0 Unported (https://creativecommons.org/licenses/by-sa/3.0/deed.en) license.

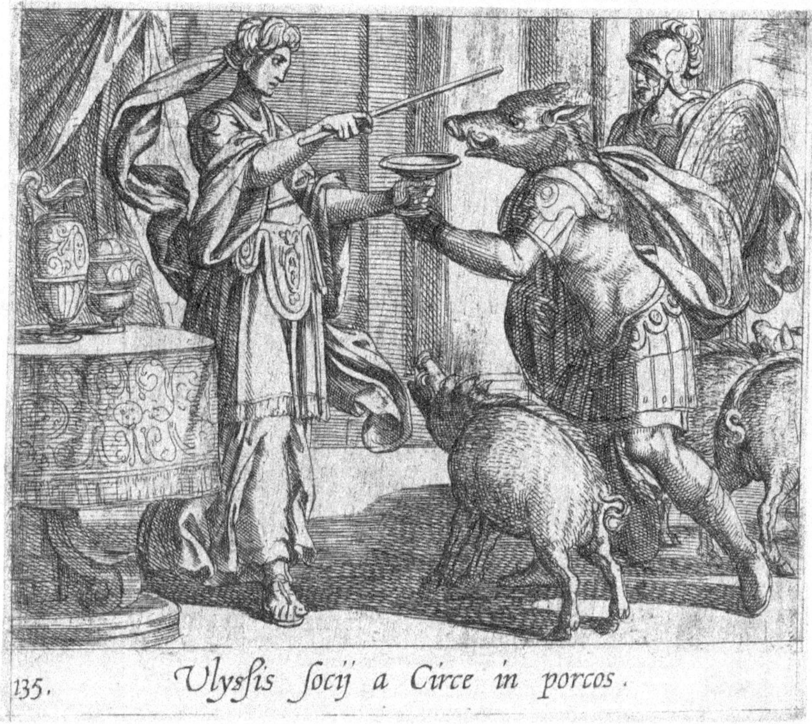

Figure 3.8 Antonio Tempesta. (1606). Etching. *Circe Changing Ulysses' Men to Swine* in Illustrations to Ovid's *Metamorphoses*.

Source: Harvard Art Museums/Fogg Museum, Gray Collection of Engravings Fund, by exchange, Accession number: S. 9. 17.17.

Despite the pelt and mask, for the humiliation of the master to be effective, Pantalone transformed has to be clearly recognized as Pantalone both by the audience and by the other characters. In Scala's Day 49, "*L'arbore incantato*," Arlechino enters transformed into a wild crane for having insulted his love. He begs and pleads and weeps, and several times stretches out his neck like a crane. His action suggests that puppetry is involved in the crane's head. Still, for our pleasure, we have to easily recognize Arlecchino.

Humans transformed into animals, by contrast to those transformed into trees, seem to provide fun not only for the audience but also for themselves. In Corsini, I/9, "*Li tre satiri*," Graziano, as a mule, Coviello as an ox, and Franceschina, as a cow, gambol, howl, bray, and moo. In Corsini I/5 "Il gran mago," Sardinello, the *zanni*, transformed into a frog, jumps in and out of the fountain.

Means of transformation

Women seem to have been transformed into trees in several ways. The actress playing one of them simply stood behind a prop tree. This kind of transformation can be seen in the illustration for Corsini I/45, "*Il Proteo*," where the nymph Filli, standing behind a small tree at right, has a headdress of leaves, and holds leaves in her outstretched arm (Figure 3.5, p. 75). Scala in, Day 49, "*L'arbore incantato*," specifies that the tree is to rotate to reveal Clori. In Locatelli II/ 21, "*Il gran mago*," Filippa comes out from within the tree. Similarly, Filli in Locatelli II/28 "*Li tre satiri*" steps out of the tree into which she has been transformed when Pantalone chops at the tree (Lea, [1934] 1962, p. 665). But sometimes the means of transformation is not evident, as in Corsini I/5 "*Il gran mago*" where, when the leaves of the tree are touched and the tree withers, Franceschina is restored to her former self. Certainly, it is not clear in the illustration for the Corsini II/8, "*La maga*" – if the watercolor is anything more than the artist's fantasy – how Filli, transformed on stage back into her prior state as a nymph, could have gotten out of the tree garb in which she is pictured (Figure 3.9, p. 83).

Transformations of characters to animals are accomplished in various ways. The character may enter already transformed, as in Locatelli II/50, "*Il Pantaloncino*" where Pantalone is led in as an ass. In Corsini I/5 "*Il gran mago*," Pantalone goes behind some bushes to eat and there is transformed into an ass while Graziano distracts the audience with his own gobbling. In one case, Locatelli I/41, "Il *Proteo*," the means of change is impossible for me to imagine: Filli, who has been taught the art of metamorphosis by her father, a magician, transforms herself for protection from sexual advances – first into a flower, and then later, into a bear and after leaping and prowling about, into a bull, and after the same performance as for the bear, into a lion roaming to and fro, and, at last, back into her own shape. Her transformations from one animal to another follow in rapid succession and apparently in full view of the audience.

In most cases, however, the change is hidden by water: in a river or, most often, in a magic fountain or well. This seems perfectly logical in that water is a symbol of both life and constant change. The flowing fountain is considered one of the principal symbols of mercury, the main agent of change in alchemical transmutation, in what was in the period under consideration, the primary age of alchemical transmutation. Water has regenerative and healing powers, analogous to those of the medieval fountain of youth, freeing the body and soul of those who bathe in or partake of it from all imperfection and bringing them back to renewed life (Ballistini, 2007, p. 336). It seems to have these very powers in the scenarios. It is also very convenient: all the character need do to be transformed is drink from the magic waters in the fountain while the actor playing him submerges his head in the well or fountain, and then, hidden from audience view, removes his mask, puts on the animal head and, in the end, returns to fully human form, by, as if drinking again, removing the animal head and replacing it with his own mask. Thus, in Locatelli II/28 "*Li tre satiri*," Gratiano and Coviello go to the fountain to drink and, in so doing, turn respectively into a mule and an ox. As animals, they dance. Subsequently, following the Magician's order to them to drink at the fountain, they are restored to their proper selves.

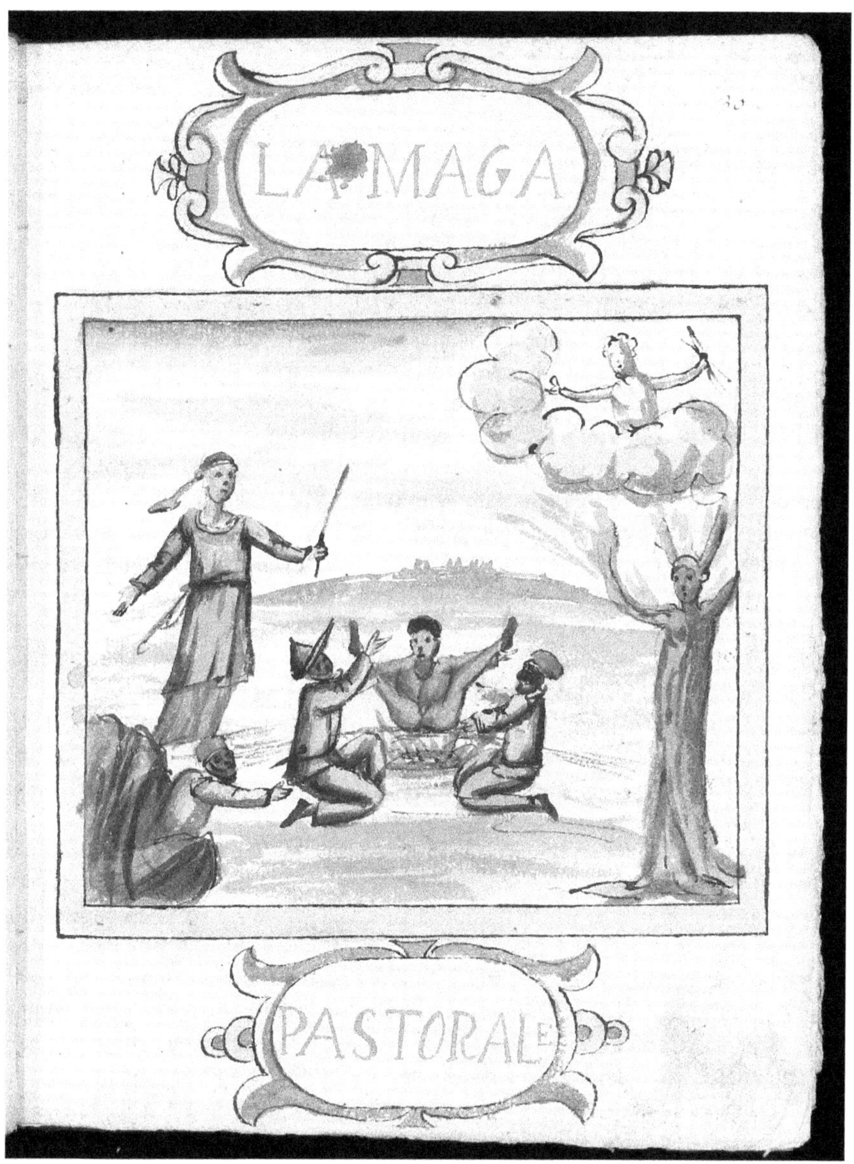

Figure 3.9 Frontispiece. "*La maga*." (n.d.). Anonymous pen and watercolor. "*Raccolta di scenari più scelti d'istrioni divisi in due volume*." MS 45.G. 6. (Biblioteca Corsiniana, Rome). Vol. I1, number 10.

Source: By permission of the Accademia Nazionale dei Lincei e Corsiniana.

In Locatelli II/50 "*Il Pantaloncino*" (Lea, [1934] 1962, p. 639), Pantalone and Olivetta, transformed into an ass and a tree respectively, are returned to their former selves when, as instructed by the Magician, the *zanni* bathe Pantalone in the fountain and, from the same fountain, water the tree. Both Pantalone and Olivetta are delighted to be restored to their former selves.

Interest of transformations

The transformations and the transformed characters were fun for the audience. But they touched far deeper than that. That the changes into animals were effected in the main with only a head, with the body left recognizable as that of the character, is perfectly logical in that the transformed beings are both animal and human at the same time. These transformations make visible a profound renaissance belief about the nature of reality. Cultural historian John Jeffries Martin explains that the self was regarded as migratory, not necessarily connected to one particular body. The body was porous and in an act of erotic or divine love, or in the case of possession, one could easily slip into another's body, or even escape from one's own. People were not bound by their skin. Within both learned and popular culture the boundaries of the self were unclear. Identity was mutable. There was no concept of a centered unitary self (Martin, 2004, pp. 18, 39, 131). Guido Ruggiero tells us the same thing: the boundaries between the material and the spiritual worlds were not clear; they were "close and permeable" (Ruggiero, 2002, p. 481).

In Corsini I/5, "*Il gran mago*," when Pantalone, transformed into an ass, eats the leaves from the tree into which Franceschina has been transformed and, on account of that, she changes back into herself, it is made explicit that the leaves, that is, Franceschina's hair, are part of her body come between the teeth of one that is "both man and not man at the same time" ("*che era huomo, et non huomo in un tempo*") (Hulfeld, 2014, p. 234).

Louise George Clubb maintains that the pastorals, unlike the comedies, tried to represent a reality not directly accessible to the physical senses, a reality of truth visible only through the eye of the mind, and that while the development of the genre of comedy over time increased their attention to the analysis of emotion and the workings of the heart, it really took the pastoral to show human "growth, change, maturation, and self-knowledge" (Clubb, 2007 p. 16).[28] "The discourse of the scenarios," observes Robert Henke "poses an implicit connection between the supernatural metamorphoses transpiring in the forest and the changes of the heart" (Henke, 2007, p. 53). That discourse shows the usefulness of the masks, in the representation of emotional transformations.

******

I have argued that masks in commedia dell'arte, broadly conceived, were a very important reason for the widespread popularity and longevity of commedia dell'arte. I have tried to show why commedia dell'arte was so influential in the history of Western theatre. Masks, along with improvisation, and acting style greatly facilitated a means of theatre production that provided for commedia dell'arte's rapid and widespread dissemination. They served to make theatre into a business. And they allowed for and enhanced the expression of observations and deeply felt beliefs about human life and, in the case of the comedies, protected the satirization of that life. It was important to these ends that the masks, in all their variety, provided a great deal of fun. The popularity and recognizability of the masks and the flexibility of improvisation greatly facilitated the spread of commedia dell'arte throughout Europe, making it there the dominant form of drama.

Notes

1 Scala's fifty scenarios constitute the oldest publication of scenarios.

2 The Corsini Collection, "*Raccolta di scenari più scelti d'istrioni divisi in due volume*" is held in the Biblioteka Accademia dei Lincei e Corsiniana, in Rome, 45. G. 5/6. For the history of the debate about the relationship between the binding of the scenarios into two volumes and the dates of their performance and transcription, see Hulfeld (2014, pp. 23–54). In the same volume Mengarelli has an essay on the watercolors serving as title pages for the scenarios (Mengarelli, 2014, pp. 117–146).

3 Twenty-three Locatelli scenarios are in print in Italian in Testaverde (2007, pp. 175–424). Six others, as well as some overlapping those in the Testaverde collection, are available in English, and some in Italian, in Lea ([1934] 1962, pp. 555–674). Ferdinando Neri ([1913], 1961) provides five pastorals, including one appearing in neither Testaverde nor Lea. Basilio Locatelli's collection itself is housed in Biblioteca Casanatense, Rome MMS 1211–12.

4 In the sixteenth and early seventeenth centuries it was felt that a room with no fourth wall was unnatural and therefore interiors were not shown on stage.

5 See especially Kerr (2015).

6 Others have also tried to express what is meant by a character mask: C.W. Marshall states that "The appearance of a stock character must connote a specific set of qualities and (more importantly) values, at first sight. These stock types need not be completely predictable, but any individuation of the character is going to be done with these initial audience expectations as a platform" (Marshall, 2006, p. 270). Antonio Fava refers to "enmasking," in which he includes not only the mask but also body, gesture, voice, speech, and language (Fava, 2007, p. 34).

7 M.A. Katriztky in her meticulous and tireless studies of commedia dell'arte iconography has found captains who wore no mask but who were readily identifiable by their flamboyant costumes, often with a metal breastplate and/or weapon, copious head and facial hair, and a generously padded codpiece. She has also found evidence of masks and veils on upper-class female characters. These masks seem to have denoted class not character. Veils, according to Katritzky, provided sexual allure and on that account their stage use was restricted. Whether veiled or not, the sexual allure of the female on stage must have been considerable. In real life, upper-class women were kept in the house because of the very danger of this allure. It was supposedly irresistible to men. And respectable women did not perform in public (Katritzky, 2007, pp. 213, 235). Ferdinanco Taviani argues that because each mask could play a variety of roles, it had no interiority (Taviani, 1985, p. 128).

8 "One way the importance of speech is shown in elite culture, at least, is in the amount of space devoted to speech in the two most famous sixteenth-century manuals of good behavior, Castiglione and Della Casa" (Burke, 1987, p. 80).

9 With an unnamed interviewer for Feats Press for Cinema.com, Helena Bonham Carter describes the extent to which, disguised as an ape, she had to depend on her voice. http://cinema.com/articles/547/planet-of-the-apes-interview-with-helena-bonham-carter.phtml (accessed 7-21-2019).

10 Hiring additional skilled actors was expensive. Scala often specifies "non-speaking" for other additional roles, as if, like roles for movie extras, they required limited skill and could be hired inexpensively in the city where the performance took place.
11 Tomaso Garzoni's *Piazza universal di tutte le professioni del mondo,* published in Venice in 1585, "conveys in a particularly lively fashion something of the chaotic, the spontaneous, and the irreverent theatricality of the public square, which he envisions as full of life and entertainments" (Martin, 2004, p. 51).
12 First Prologue to *Il finto marito,* in Scala, 1976, p. 198.
13 Adolescence continued to age 25, youth until age 40. Old age began at 40 or 45 (Creighton, 1967, pp. 12–13 and *passim).*
14 In the first Prologue of seven pages, Scala uses the word "imitation," meaning imitation of nature, fourteen times (Scala, Marotti, 1976, p. cx).
15 For tragedy, Vitruvious specified columns, pediments, statues, and other royal decorations.
16 It is worth noting that prop lists specified clothing for a Jew, a gypsy, a crazy person, a charcoal seller, a slave, a magician, a duke, a merchant, a locksmith, a mail carrier, a porter, a barber, a lady, a Turk, a captain, a farmer, a traveler, a spirit, a shadow, and others, making clear the extent that the role or profession of each person could be identified by his or her clothing.
17 Orgel (2014, p. 460) argues that few symbols on the Renaissance stage would have been left unexplained by language.
18 I have found Stemp (2006) on symbolism in Italian Renaissance art helpful.
19 See Fordham University's online *Modern History Sourcebook* (Halsall, 1999). "All books and writings dealing with geomancy, hydromancy, aeromancy, pyromancy, oneiromancy, chiromancy, necromancy, or with sortilege, mixing of poisons, augury, auspices, sorcery, magic arts, are absolutely repudiated."
20 Surtz (1996, p. 85) makes very clear that devils were masked.
21 So ubiquitous was magic that Kathryn A. Edwards (2015) simply uses *Everyday Magic in Early Modern Europe* as the title for her collection of essays on the subject, suggesting an activity we are to take for granted.
22 Butterworth (1998) explains the use of fire, how it was provided, and the dangers in providing it on stage in early English and Scottish theatre. Katritzky (2014, pp. 368–369) notes that "fire, fireworks and devils have a venerable stage tradition from the time of medieval mystery plays onwards."
23 See also: Corsini, I/21, II/48, and II/50.
24 See for instance: Henke (1997, pp. 16–18) and Sampson (2006b, p. 4). For further accounts of the subject matter of pastoral drama, see also Schneider (2010), Walker (1987), and Niccoli (1989).
25 According to Lisa Sampson, the poetic forms used in the scripted pastorals were a combination of *endecasillabi* and *settenari* (Sampson, 2006a, p. 93).
26 Instances in which the prop lists include a forest, make it conceivable that the forest could be transported and the less elaborate of the pastorals played before a popular street audience. But the elaborate and unique scenic effects required in the majority of pastorals I have examined in Corsini and Locatelli, and their costumes requirements would probably have made street performance uncommon.
27 Corsini, I/25 "*Il pozzo,*" is a comedy set in the city, which, in addition to having a well with silver in the bottom, a grotto, a magician, and a devil, also has a wildman. It is another of the anomalous comedies discussed earlier.
28 Clubb has consistently gone further, claiming that the written pastorals reveal "a pattern of higher meaning that accords with the providential plan of a divinity." In this, the transformations would seem to play an important role. Clubb acknowledges, however, that the larger signifying function seen in the written drama is not self-evident in the scenarios, which reveal only the genre and theatregrams of pastoral. She is able to point to a sonnet appended to a play from 1584, written by an actor and showing clear

signs of the influence of commedia dell'arte: Bartolomeo Rossi's *Flammella pastorale*, which praises the scenario's demonstration of the workings of human blindness and of heavenly providence (Clubb, 2007, p. 20). How much weight we should give to that finding, I do not know. Clubb does observe that it is evidence that at least some professional actors sought the critical respect of the literati.

Works cited

Aasted, Elsebeth. (1992). "What the Corsini Scenari Can Tell Us about the *Commedia dell'arte*." In *Analecta Romana Instituti Danici*. Vol 20, pp. 159-82.

Alberti, Carmelo, ed. (1996). *Gli scenari Correr: La commedia dell'arte a Venezia*. (Rome: Bulzoni).

Andrews, Richard. (2008). *The Commedia dell'arte of Flaminio Scala: A Translation and Analysis of 30 Scenarios*. Edited and translated by Richard Andrews. (Lanham, MD: Scarecrow Press).

Ballistini, Matilde. (2007). *Astrology, Magic, and Alchemy in Art*. (Los Angeles, CA: J. Paul Getty Museum).

Baratay, Eric and Elisabeth Hardouin-Fugier. (2002). *Zoo: A History of Zoological Gardens in the West*. (London: Reaktion Books).

Barish, Jonas. (1981). *The Antitheatrical Prejudice*. (Berkeley: University of California Press).

Briccio, Giovanni. (1676). *La Rosmira*. (Roma: Francesco Tizzoni). Available in Google Books.

Brook, Peter. (1987). *The Shifting Point: Forty Years of Theatrical Exploration, 1946–1987*. (New York: Harper and Row).

Burckhardt, Jacob. (1904). *Civilization of the Renaissance in Italy*. Translated by Ludwig Geiger. (London: S. Sonnenshein).

Burke, Peter. ([1987], 2005). *Historical Anthropology of Modern Italy: Essays on Perception and Communication*. (New York: Cambridge University Press).

Butterworth, Philip. (1998). *Theatre of Fire: Special Effects in Early English and Scottish Theatre*. (London: Society for Theatre Research).

Clubb, Louise George. (1989). *Italian Drama in Shakespeare's Time*. (New Haven, CT: Yale University Press).

Clubb, Louise George. (2007). "Pastoral Jazz from the Writ to the Liberty." In *Italian Culture in the Drama of Shakespeare and his Contemporaries: Rewriting, Remaking, Refashioning*, edited by Michele Marrapodi, pp. 15–26. (Burlington, VT: Ashgate).

Cohen, Elizabeth Storr and Thomas Vance Cohen. (2001). *Daily Life in Renaissance Italy*. (Westport, CT: Greenwood Press).

Creighton, Gilbert. (1967). "When Did a Man in the Renaissance Grow Old?" *Studies in the Renaissance* 14: pp. 7–32.

de'Sommi, Leone. ([1556] 1968). *Quattro dialoghi in materia di rappresentazioni sceniche*. Edited by Ferruccio Marotti. (Milano: Il Polifilo).

Edwards, Kathryn A. (2015). *Everyday Magic in Early Modern Europe*. (Burlington, VT: Ashgate).

Fava, Antonio. (2007). *The Comic Mask in the Commedia dell'Arte: Actor Training, Improvisation, and the Poetics of Survival*. (Evanston, IL: Northwestern University Press).

Ferber, Sarah. (2015). "The Constitution and Conditions of Everyday Magic in Late Medieval and Early Modern Catholic Europe." In *Everyday Magic in Early Modern Europe*, edited by Kathryn A. Edwards, pp. 161–180. (Burlington, VT: Ashgate).

Freedman, Luba. (2011). *Classical Myths in Italian Renaissance Painting*. (Cambridge: Cambridge University Press).

Fulchignoni, Enrico. (1990). "Oriental Influences on the *Commedia dell'Arte*." Translated by Una Crowley. *Asian Theatre Journal* 71 (1): pp. 29–41.

Gentilcore, David. (2006). *Medical Charlatanism in Early Modern Italy*. (Oxford: Oxford University Press).

Guarini, Battista. (1602). *Il pastor fido*. (Venice: Giovanni Battista Ciotti).

Gurr, Andrew. (1980). *The Shakespearean Stage 1574–1642*. (Cambridge: Cambridge University Press).

Halsall, Paul. (1999). "Council of Trent: Ten Rules Concerning Prohibited Books Drawn Up by the Fathers Chosen by the Council of Trent and Approved by Pope Pius [1] IX." *Modern History Sourcebook*, Fordham University. https://sourcebooks.fordham.edu/halsall/mod/trent-booksrules.asp (Accessed August 28, 2018).

Henke, Robert. (1997). *Pastoral Transformations: Italian Tragicomedy and Shakespeare's Late Plays*. (Newark: University of Delaware Press).

Henke, Robert. (2007). "Transporting Tragicomedy: Shakespeare and the Magic Pastoral of *Commedia dell'Arte*." In *Early Modern Tragicomedy*, edited by Subja Mukherji and Raphael Lyne, pp. 43–58. (Suffolk, UK: Boydell and Brewer).

Hulfeld, Stefan. (2014). *Scenari più scelti d'istrioni: Italienisch-Deutsche Edition der einhundert Commedia all'improvviso-Scenarien aus der Sammlung Corsiniana*. (2 vols). (Vienna: V & R Unipress).

Ingegneri, Angelol (1989) *Della poesia rappresentativa* (Ferrara: Instituto di Studi Rinascimentali)

Johnson, James H. (2011). *Venice Incognito: Masks in the Serene Republic*. (Berkeley: University of California Press).

Katritzky, M.A. (1998). "Was *Commedia dell'Arte* Performed by Mountebanks?" *Theatre Research International* 23 (2): pp. 104–125.

Katritzky, M.A. (2006). *The Art of Commedia: A Study in the Commedia dell'Arte 1560–1620 with Special Reference to the Visual Records*. (Amsterdam: Rodopi).

Katritzky, M.A. (2007). *Women, Medicine and Theatre, 1500–1750: Literary Mountebanks and Quacks*. (Aldershot, England: Ashgate).

Katritzky, M.A. (2014). "Comic Stage Routines in Guarinonius' Medical Treatise of 1610." In *European Theatre Performance in Practice, 1580–1750*, edited by Robert Henke and M.A Katritzky, pp. 363–378. (Burlington, VT: Ashgate).

Kerr, Rosalind. (2015). *The Rise of the Diva on the Sixteenth-Century Commedia dell'Arte Stage*. (Toronto, ON: University of Toronto Press).

Lea, Kathleen M. ([1934] 1962). *Italian Popular Comedy: A Study in the Commedia dell'Arte, 1560–1620 with Special Reference to the English Stage*. (2 vols). (New York: Russell and Russell).

Machiavelli, Niccolò. ([1532] 2008). *The Prince*. Translated with an introduction by James B. Atkinson. (Indianapolis, Ind.: Hackett).

Marshall, C.W. (2006). *The Stagecraft and Performance of Roman Comedy*. (Cambridge: Cambridge University Press).

Martin, John Jeffries. (2004). *Myths of Renaissance Individualism*. (New York: Palgrave).

Mengarelli, Stefano. (2014). "Le kolorierten Federzeichnungen der Scenari più scelti d'istrioni." In *Scenari più scelti d'istrioni: Italienisch-Deutsche Edition der einhundertommedia all'improvviso-Szenarien aus der Sammlung Corsiniana*, edited and translated by Stefan Hulfeld, vol. 1, pp. 117–146. (Vienna: V & R Unipress).

Neri, Ferdinando. (1913). *Scenari delle marshere in Arcadia*. (Castello: S. Lapi).

Niccoli, G.A. (1989). *Cupid, Satyr, and the Golden Age: Pastoral Dramatic Scenes of the Late Renaissance*. (New York: Lang).

Orgel, Stephen. (1996). *Impersonations: The Performance of Gender in Shakespeare's England.* (Cambridge: Cambridge University Press).

Orgel, Stephen. (2014). "Theaters and Audiences." In *European Theatre Performance Practice*, 1580–1750, edited by Robert Henke and M.A. Katritzky, pp. 437–472. (Burlington, VT: Ashgate).

Pandolfi, Vito. (1957-1961). *Commedia dell'arte: Storia e testi.* (6 vol.). (Florence: Sansoni).

Perrucci, Andre. ([1699] 2008). *A Treatise on Acting, From Memory and by Improvisation 1699.* Bilingual edition. Edited and translated by Francesco Cotticelli, Anne Goodrich Heck, and Thomas F. Heck. (Lanham, MD: Scarecrow Press).

Pietropaolo, Domenico. (2001). "The Theatre." In *Harlequin Unmasked: The Commedia Dell'Arte and Porcelain Sculpture*, edited by Meredith Chilton, pp. 19–32. (New Haven, CT: George R. Gardiner Museum of Ceramic Art with Yale University Press).

Ruggiero, Guido. (2002). *A Companion to the Worlds of the Renaissance*. (Oxford: Blackwell).

Sampson, Lisa. (2006a). "Pastoral Drama." In *A History of Italian Theatre*, edited by Joseph Farrell and Paolo Puppa, pp. 91–101. (Cambridge: Cambridge University Press).

Sampson, Lisa. (2006b). *Pastoral Drama in Early Modern Italy: The Making of a New Genre*. (London: Legenda, Modern Humanities Research Association and Maney Publishing).

Saslow, James M. (1996). *The Medici Wedding of 1589*. (New Haven, CT: Yale University Press).

Scala, Flamino. ([1967] 1989). *Scenarios of the commedia dell'Arte: Flaminio Scala's Il teatro delle favole rappresentative* Edited and translated by Henry F. Salerno. (New York: Limelight).

Scala, Flamino. (1976). *Il teatro delle favole rappresentative*. Edited by Ferruccio Marotti. (Rome: Il Polifilo).

Scala, Flaminio. (2008). *The Commedia dell'arte of Flaminio Scala: A Translation and Analysis of 30 Scenarios*. Edited and translated by Richard Andrews. (Lanham, MD: Scarecrow Press).

Schneider, Federico. (2010). *Pastoral Drama and Healing in Early Modern Italy*. (Burlington, VT: Ashgate).

Schmitt, Natalie Crohn. (2014). *Befriending the Commedia dell'Arte of Flaminio Scala.* (Toronto, ON: University of Toronto Press).

Sidnell, Michael J. (1991). *Sources of Dramatic Theory I: Plato to Congreve*. (Cambridge: Cambridge University Press).

Jon R. (2012) *Dissimulation ahd the Culture of Secrecy in Early Modern Europe*. (Berkeley: University of California Press).

Stemp, Richard. (2006). *The Secret Language of the Renaissance: Decoding the Hidden Symbolism in Italian Art*. (London: Duncan Baird).

Surtz, Ronald E. (1996). "Masks in the Medieval Peninsular Theatre." In *Festive Drama: Papers from the Sixth Triennial Colloquium of the International Society for the Study of Medieval Theatre (Lancaster, July, 1989)*, edited by Meg Twycross, pp. 80–87. (Cambridge: D.S. Brewer).

Taviani, Ferdinado. (1985). "Positions du masque dans la commedia dell'arte." In *Le masque du rite au théâtre*, edited by Odette Asland and Denis Bablet, pp. 119–134. (Paris: Centre national de la recherche scientifique).

Testaverde, Anna Maria, ed. (2007). *I canovacci della commedia dell'arte*. (Turin: Giulio Einaudi).

Twycross, Meg and Sarah Carpenter. (2002). *Masks and Masking in Medieval and Early Tudor England*. (Burlington, VT: Ashgate).

Vitruvious. (1826). *The Architecture of M. Vitruvius Pollio in Ten Books*. Translated by Joseph Gwilt. (London: Priestly & Weale). Available on Google.

Walker, S.F. (1987). *A Cure for Love: A Generic Study of the Pastoral Idyll*. (New York: Garland).

Wiles, David. (1991). *Masks of Menander*. (Cambridge: Cambridge University Press).

Wiles, David. (2007). *Mask and Performance in Greek Tragedy: From Ancient Festival to Modern Experimentation*. (New York: Cambridge University Press).

4 Coda

Commedia dell'arte today

A 2015 collection of essays, otherwise generally endorsing the idea of the continuity of a commedia dell'arte tradition from its origin to the present day, includes a wayward essay by Giulia Filacanapa asserting that such continuity is largely fictitious.[1] Commedia dell'arte, Filacanapa believes, essentially died in the eighteenth century. Twenty-first century commedia dell'arte, she states, using Eric Hobsbawm's phrase, is an "invented tradition," a myth (2015, pp. 379–380).

The idea of commedia dell'arte as an invented tradition gets considerably more play in a 2018 collection of essays. One of the book's editors, Daniele Vianello, in her introduction to the collection entitled *Commedia dell'Arte in Context*, explains that the book is divided into two parts "History" and "Myth and Reception" (Vianello, 2018, pp. 4, 8). The operative assumption of the contributors is neatly expressed by contributor Renzo Guardenti:

> the last years of the eighteenth century saw the end . . . of the commedia dell'arte. The ideological and productive contexts which had allowed it to develop and thrive on the European scene for over two hundred years had, by this time, disappeared.
>
> (Guardenti, 2018, p. 221)

One of the collection's editors, Christopher Balme, in his conclusion to the collection, observes that a number of very skilled commedia dell'arte performers, teachers, and scholars, generally expressing concern about the lack of interest in commedia in Italy itself, have applied to the United Nations Education, Scientific, and Cultural Organization (UNESCO) for recognition of commedia dell'arte as an intangible cultural heritage.[2] In order to gain such recognition, every application must make clear, among other things, he explains, how the art form in question provides communities and groups with "a sense of identity and continuity" (Balme, 2018, p. 312). Balme argues against UNESCO's recognition for commedia dell'arte because, he says, while commedia has undoubtedly had great transnational cultural and historical impact on theatre (and I would add on art, music, dance, and film), its practice has lacked the required historical continuity and that, further, it was and is simply too diverse to meet UNESCO's emphasis on regionality, particularity, and community (pp. 313–314). Vianello, another editor, in her introduction to the volume, and Erika Fisher-Lichte, in an essay included in the volume, like Balme and Filacanapa, call the commedia dell'arte that has so powerfully influenced and continues to influence directors, teachers, and theatre groups a "myth" (Vianello, 2018, pp. 8–13; Fisher-Lichte, 2018, p. 216).[3]

Several things, other than the arguments that Balme has presented, prohibit commedia dell'arte from being an intangible cultural heritage that provides a sense of identity and continuity:

1 The comic scenarios speak powerfully to the ethos of the period in which they were performed. But today most all of the issues addressed seem dated, at least in the West: loyalty and obedience to the father as a matter of his honor and that of the house, the utmost importance to the well-to-do of arranged marriages, the restriction of unmarried upper-class women to the house in order to protect their chastity, and the treachery and trickery of servants. And while it would be extremely interesting to see a pastoral scenario, replete with nymphs, gods, devils, and seventeenth-century magical effects, it would not be interesting to see very many of them.
2 The information about performance provided in the scenarios, in published speeches, and in the iconography is limited. This, despite the fact, as I argue here, and in more detail in my *Befriending the Commedia dell'Arte of Flaminio Scala* (2014), that one can go much further in the reconstruction of the performance of scenarios, particularly of the Scala scenarios, than has been previously thought; despite the fact that Vito Pandolfi's multi-volume collection (1957–1961) provides a generous sample of speeches and of plays mimicking commedia dell'arte; that M.A. Katritzky, particularly in her *The Art of Commedia* (2006) has extensively and rewardingly examined commedia's iconography; and that most recently, as I have shown in Chapter 2, Emily Wilbourne (2016) has led us to some understanding of the sound of commedia dell'arte. Given all that, the scenarios remain on the page as just that – outlines of actions.
3 The most serious problem in providing a sense of continuity in the performance of commedia dell'arte is its language. As I argue in Chapter 1, its performance was part of a long rhetorical tradition, a tradition that is lost today. To give some idea of the problem, I quote in part from a translation provided by Julie Campbell (2002) of *La Mirtilla*, a pastoral. *La Mirtilla* is the only play written by the famed commedia *innamorata*, Isabella Andreini. Filli's lament, *Act 1, Scene 2*, although it likely has more pastoral references than a lament in a comedy, gives an idea of what, ideally, a lament common to both pastoral and comic scenarios was like. Keep in mind that in performance of a scenario the lament would have been improvised or semi-improvised – in the tragedies and pastorals, in verse.

In the play, Filli, a nymph, loves Uranio, a shepherd, who in turn loves Ardelia, a nymph who is a follower of Diana, the Roman goddess who swore never to marry.

Filli speaks:

> Sometimes I think about
> my formerly happy state which was equal to any other's,
> and now more than any other's
> it is weary and full of tedious worries!
> Then sorrow afflicts and vexes me,
> and desperation induces me (alas)
> to desire death.
> O, Filli, more unfortunate than any other!
> You surely know, O forests,
> valleys, woods, and fields,
> what my life is like, because so often
> you hear me complain, and the winds also
> know, for, listening to my sharp pain,
> they often pause.
> Then I, so unfortunate – while the stars
> decorate the beautiful night sky,
> and Cynthia[4] alights in the embrace
> of her beloved youth, and the night spreads its dark veil,
> and sleep and silence offer tired mortals
> their deserved repose – I go out alone
> without fear of a horrid encounter
> with nocturnal ghosts. Miserable and lost
> in the lonely forests and desolate fields,
> I call to Uranio in vain. When I demand of
> heaven if it will always be so unmerciful to me,
> Echo, who always responds to my speech
> from the rocky hollows, increases my torment.
> Thus I disturb the night of its faithful silence
> with solemn cries of woe, and while I cry,
> I hear night birds, whose screeching
> brings me a sign of bad luck.
> And living in such death, I see the stars
> vanish one by one, until only
> the amorous star remains in the sky.
> While it belatedly departs from me,
> I humbly pray that it puts some end
> to my misfortune; otherwise, I
> will become a bitter Parca[5] to myself.
> [and so on, languishing for another page]
>
> (Andreini, [1588] 2002, pp. 20–21)[6]

Maria Luisa Doglio, in her introduction to her edition of *La Mirtilla*, calls attention to Andreini's use of Virgil, Ovid, Petrarch, and others throughout the work

(1995, pp. 9–10). Anne MacNeil notes, in general, Andrieni's rhetorical fluency, her allusions to classical authors, and her comic wit (MacNeil, 2003, pp. 36–37). No performer today can improvise such stuff, and an audience would tire of it and of a whole play much of it in such elaborated language.

While the lovers had the most high-flown and literary speech, the doctor in comedy would deliver long pontifications full of mangled Latin, for the appreciation of those who knew Latin and, for the audience in general, he provided an endless flow of distortions, malapropisms, and weighty pronouncements like "someone who is asleep cannot be awake"; and "someone without legs will have trouble walking." Francesco Andreini, the most famous performer of the braggart captain, published a book of his captain's boasts (Andreini, ([1607] 1987). They make clear what such boasts at their best were like. They go on for pages and are full of frequent allusions to classical mythology and personified abstractions that, like the langague of the *innamorati* would have been partially memorized and partially improvised. To make matters more difficult, the lovers, who spoke Tuscan interacted with the doctor, who spoke Bolognese, and with the Spanish captain, as well as with Pantalone, and the servants, each with their own distinct dialects, dialects that seem to have been an important part of the comedy.

Today, most actors do not have a vast store of memorized material at the ready. They do not have notebooks filled with proverbs, similes, and maxims; they are not imbued with *sententiae*, descriptions, examples, comparisons, and Ciceronean figures; and they cannot recite Petrarch by heart, nor, for that matter, any more recent author. They cannot improvise laments and love duets full of metaphors. They lack the gestures and vocalization, and collectively they cannot improvise the very different dialects.

This is not at all to deny that commedia dell'arte, however variously interpreted, has been an extremely important influence on twentieth-century theatre. A list of some of the important directors and performers each of whom claims to have been inspired by commedia dell'arte, as usefully provided by Vianello, includes Jean-Louis Barrault Jacques Copeau, Gordon Craig, Charles Dullin, Nikolai Evreinov, Louis Jouvet, Marcel Marceau, Vsevolod Meyerhold, Sergei Radlov, Max Reinhardt, Konstantin S. Stanislavski, Alexandr Tairov, Yevgeny Vakhtangov, and – more recently – Eugenio Barba, Benno Besson, Eduardo de Filippo, Dario Fo, Jacques Lecoq, Ariane Mnouchkine, Giovanni Poli, and Giorgio Strehler (Vianello, 2018, p. 10).

Each, seeking to reinvent theatre, appears to have been inspired by a different understanding of commedia dell'arte, each, in effect, implementing his or her own idea of what commedia was: variously, a fully collective creation, a new work each night created *ex nihilo*, freed of the tyranny of an author, of a text, of realism, of technology and expense, a popular street theatre, filled with happiness and the joy of life, intimate with its audience, employing masks to free the actor from self-consciousness and psychology, and emphasizing bodily movement including acrobatics and clowning over a verbal component.

The most successful American groups claiming to be inspired by commedia dell'arte with which I am familiar make no attempt to reproduce it but, rather, freely adapt it for their own purposes along with a variety of other theatrical forms. They are the San Francisco Mime Troupe, begun in 1959 and El Teatro Campesino, begun in 1965. Internationally, probably the most famous existing group, Théâtre du Soleil, founded in 1964, I have regrettably seen only on YouTube. Amazingly, all these groups have been in existence between fifty and sixty years. Over the long period of their existence, each has been very well-documented.

An early unsigned program note from a production of Théâtre du Soleil serves, in effect, to explain the goals of each of the theatres:

> We want to reinvent the rules of the game that unveil daily reality by showing it not as familiar and immutable, but as surprising and transformable. This will thus be a theatre directly taken from social reality, which is not mere observation, but rather encouragement to change the conditions in which we live.
>
> (Cixous, 2016, p. xiii)

"The goal of Théâtre du Soleil," writes Cixous editor Lara Stevens, who might as well be speaking for all three groups, is "to reveal to spectators the possibility of altering contemporary conditions of inequality and injustice" (Cixous, 2016, p. xiv). Logically, given their political leanings, the three groups all began as collectives, albeit with very strong leaders, and they used group improvisation in their playwrighting.

San Francisco Mime Troupe

The San Francisco Mime Troupe, founded and originally directed by R.G. Davis in 1959 takes its free shows to parks and community centers, primarily in the San Francisco Bay Area, but has also performed both nationally and internationally enabled by their characteristic rough and ready design elements that allow it to function economically and to set up for performance anywhere in a few hours. Over time, and with changing leadership, the group has become more ethnically diverse and more feminist in its outlook, and it often casts against ethnic and gender type. The players seek to attract a wide and varied audience for the always political topics they take on by presenting them in the context of satirical musical comedy. They believe that laughter not only makes the material acceptable but also brings audience members together (Orenstein, 2006, p. 183). Seeking to point out the social constructedness of roles, they theatricalize them presenting exaggerated types, played with large gesture, in forms inspired by commedia dell'arte and by vaudeville, circus, melodrama, comic books, and television sitcoms (Orenstein, 2006, p. 187). Believing in, calling on, and seeking to empower their audiences to address the issues they bring to attention, the conclusion of their works is always uplifting. Not surprisingly, the group was originally attracted to, not only the techniques of commedia performance, but also to its examination of power relationships between masters and servants. They continue to use improvisation in devising their works.

Salaries, which most troupe members need to supplement with outside work, are decided upon collectively. Funds are provided by passing the hat after performances and through public funding, which the group accepted, after much debate, as necessary to offering free performances, but that troupe members continually fear will compromise their work (Orenstein, 2006, p. 190).

A list of the San Francisco Mime Troupe's recent annual musicals gives a good idea of that work: *Seeing Red: A Time Traveling Musical* (2018) about the history and hope offered by socialism in the United States; *The Wall* (2017), featuring a U.S. Immigration and Customs Enforcement officer; *School* (2016), about the failure of mixing for profit and public education; *Freedom Land* (2015), about the police in the United States and its treatment of minorities.

El Teatro Campesino

In 1965, Luis Valdez, founded El Teatro Campesino (farmworkers theatre) after having performed for a year with the San Francisco Mime troupe, where he was introduced to agitprop and commedia dell'arte. Initially, El Teatro Campesino performers were indeed farmworkers who, with their performances, were seeking to raise support for the United Farm Workers union. They performed *actos* (short satirical skits developed through improvisation that capitalized on the Mexican oral tradition). They brought their work to the fields in which Chicanos were working by performing alongside the fields on flatbed trucks.

In 1967, the then larger group with more skilled performers expanded its focus to include the plight of urban Chicanos and to infighting within the Chicano movement. Out of necessity, their performances embraced *rasquachismo*, a making-do with what they had or could find – a tactic all too familiar to Chicanos in everyday life. Even El Teatro's language, Spanglish, exemplified *rasquachismo*. Its presentational style employed masks and broad acting. In 1971 Valdez published a selection of the group's *actos* for free use in any way by interested groups.

Over time, the Teatro also expanded the kinds of performances it did to include *mitos* – enactments of indigenous mythologies, using over-sized masks, to reaffirm the heritage of the Chicanos, *corredos* – narrative ballads – and *carpa* – vaudeville and carnival inspired by early twentieth-century Mexican tent shows. The performances were designed to show that the way forward was through self-respect, and unified action.[7]

In 1980, with the fame and financial success of Valdez's scripted play *Zoot Suit* (which gained its force from the earlier collective work), Valdez took over El Teatro Campesino from the collective, along with its name, and made it into a professional theatre under his direction. Today, one of his sons serves as its director. El Teatro produces Valdez's plays, but also those of resident playwrights; it revives old pieces that had been developed collectively (and are unfortunately still politically relevant); and it collectively develops new works focused on the Chicano community. It has its own permanent theatre, a repurposed packing-house, in a farming community in California's central valley, San Juan Battista (population 1,975, half of which is Chicano). It also takes its productions elsewhere, particularly in California, where it can attract a Chicano audience. Valdez's plays, under the son's direction and otherwise, are frequently performed in major professional theatres. His newest work, *Valley of the Heart*, about uncertainty and turmoil in the farmlands for both Chicano and Japanese families after the bombing of Pearl Harbor, employing both Japanese and Chicano actors, played in 1918, at the well-known Mark Taper Forum in Los Angeles. The company's annual Christmas Pageant was, in 2018, Luis Valdez's adaptation of the story of the four apparitions of Our Lady of Guadalupe to the indigenous messenger Juan Diego in 1531. It was a celebration, entirely in Spanish, performed in the home theatre in San Juan Batista, using live music and Aztec dance, continuing Valdez's interest in raising the self-respect of Chicanos.

Jorge Huerta, a long-time scholar of El Teatro Campesino, and of Chicano theatre in general, claims that all Latino theatre including community, student, and professional theatre companies, individual theatre artists, and filmmakers owe their existence, directly or indirectly to Luis Valdez and the Teatro Campesino. Its aesthetic and political legacies continue to hold sway over presentations by these groups in the United States and even abroad. "The Teatro lives in the continuing work of so many people who passed through the troupe's cultural centers. It lives in the people who participated in workshops conducted by Teatro members either at home or on tour" (Huerta, 2015).

The Théâtre du Soleil

Ariane Mnouchkine, the long-time director of Théâtre du Soleil, studied with Jacques Lacoq, who was explicitly influenced by commedia dell'arte. Her company, generously subsidized by the French government, as of 2005, had "seventy-five members from thirty-five countries, speaking twenty-two different languages" (Miller, 2007, p. 14). Members of the collective are paid equally. They can afford to put on lavishly costumed plays, with music especially composed for them. And, when they perform a written play, it is sometimes newly translated for them. Even when the group is working with scripted plays, as it sometimes does, rather than devising plays from the beginning, it relies heavily on research and on improvisation in developing characters and acting styles. Work on a production, whether scripted in advance or developed through collective improvisation, can go on for a very extended period of time.

Play texts, derived from group improvisation on a chosen topic, are presently edited into more coherent form by the writer and long-term collaborator, Hélène Cixous, a renowned, feminist, philosopher, cultural commentator, and playwright. As titles of past plays, in English, suggest, Théâtre du Soleil may engage topics that are very ambitious and further afield than those of the Mime Troupe or El Teatro, like *The Last Caravan Stop*, about patterns of immigration throughout the world, or *The Terrible but Unsuccessful History of Norodom Sihanouk, King of Cambodia*, or *Drums on the Dam*, about China.

In keeping with her mentor, Jacques Lecoq, who believed that masks best served to externalize expression of the internal, Mnouchkine relies heavily on mask work – even in developing productions that do not finally use masks. In addition to having been influenced by commedia dell'arte, Mnouchine has been strongly influence by East Asian and South Asian theatre movements including their music, costumes, masks, puppets, make-up and acting and may use them, among other ways, to provide a Brechtian distance in performance even of Western fully-scripted plays, which she otherwise follows verbatim. In performance, actors may be masked and may play a variety of roles, sometimes against gender and ethnic types, sometimes as puppets, "often playing 'universal' rather than individualized characters" (Wilmer, 2018, p. 174).

Members of the group, even though they no longer live together as in the past, continue to promote a collective spirit by working together on all aspects of the enterprise, including cooking and cleaning. To promote that collective spirit and a sense of ritual in the audience, they may invite the audience to peer into their dressing rooms to watch them getting into make-up and may serve food to the audience that they themselves prepared.

Théâtre du Soleil performs, in an old munitions factory outside Paris that they made into a large theatre. Members redesign the space and lighting for each show. Given the specifically designed space and lighting for each performance and the large multinational cast, the group does not often travel. Nonetheless, it is regarded as one of the most innovative and well-known theatres in the world. The workshops it offers are highly sought after.

While both the Mime troupe and the El Teatro are now led by other than their originators, Mnouchkine, almost 80, still provides the visionary leadership for Théâtre du Soleil. Unlike the work of the Mime Troupe and the Teatro, which often deliberately present a kind of thrown-together aesthetic, the work of Théâtre du Soleil is meticulously orchestrated, choreographed, staged, designed, lit, and costumed. It is – to judge from selections of their performances on YouTube – gorgeous.

The Improvised Shakespeare Company

Markedly different from the three groups I just described is a group I have seen many times in Chicago where I live: The Improvised Shakespeare Company (ISC).[8] It is not at all political and makes no claim to having been influenced by commedia dell'arte. Yet the group, founded by Blain Swen in 2005, seems more closely connected to commedia dell'arte, at least in spirit, than any group with which I am familiar. Perhaps unknown to ISC performers, it is, in fact, a fourth-generation descendant of a group founded in 1955 by David Shepherd because he was inspired by commedia dell'arte.

Shepherd's idea was to have actors improvise short skits based on scenarios reflecting situations in contemporary society. He teamed up with Paul Sills, who was influenced by his mother Viola Spolin's improvisational games with children at Jane Addams' settlement house in Chicago. The group they formed took the name Compass Players, after the Chicago bar in which they performed. In 1959, renamed Second City, the group moved into its own space. By this time, the ensemble was still performing short skits based on improvisational material but these had been carefully polished and rehearsed. Del Close, who had been a director at Second City, was asked by Charna Halpern in 1981 to help her with her newly formed group, then called the Improv Olympics, subsequently I.O. Close's idea was to develop fully improvised full-length pieces, with each performance based upon a title offered by an audience member attending that evening's performance and then never performed again. After some experimentation, Halpern and Close settled on a form arbitrarily called the "Harold," in which relatively independent themes based on a title provided by an audience member at the onset of that performance, were established in the first act and then brought back and interwoven in the second, and then finally brought all together in a conclusion.

In 2005, using essentially the form of the Harold, Swen, after some experimentation with improvising Shakespeare in Los Angeles, formed The Improvised Shakespeare Company with performers trained in the Harold at I.O., and in other of Chicago's innumerable improv venues in addition to Second City, as he himself had been. Swen, essentially a *capocomico*, conducts a workshop for the ISC actors in Shakespearean language (they have vocabulary quizzes), in the use of metaphors and similes, and in heightening the emotions expressed. Actors study Shakespeare films and read Shakespeare's plays. The group, presently eighteen male actors selected by Swen, performs with a rotating cast of five with each actor playing multiple roles, both male and female and sometimes animal. There are no programs, actors are not introduced by name, and they vary from performance to performance. Paid a nominal amount, most supplement their incomes with theatre teaching or writing. Many perform in other of Chicago's very numerous improv groups as well. In performance, the upper-class characters, witches, and fairies aim to speak in iambic pentameter. In practice the actors often rhyme considerably more than Shakespeare in iambic lines of varying lengths. The end rhyme may be something that has a contemporary as well as a period reference.

In 1995, Charna Halpern, then on her own, moved out from above the bar where I.O. performances had taken place to a very large space she had purchased just in time in a rapidly revitalizing commercial area. In this space the ISC rents one of the four theatres for five performances a week, Thursday through Saturday. The space seats 185, has a shallow stage, three curtained openings, two openings with no curtains, and two windows with shutters, to which the ISC adds four metal folding chairs that they use in any number of ways. Concurrently, five other company members travel nationally and occasionally internationally in various venues for about a hundred days of the year.

Like Second City, Compass Players, and I.O. before it, given the theatre's origins in a bar, and its continuance in I.O.s space, the ISC performances in Chicago are cabaret style. Drinks and bar food can be ordered both before the performance and during the single intermission. The performance lasts an hour and a half including the intermission. Ticket price is presently twenty dollars, but even with food and drink as extras, this is a relatively inexpensive night out: there is no food or drink minimum. Audience members appear to be mostly in their twenties, white, and college educated. Many come in small groups rather than as couples. Some of the five performances a week regularly sell out. I suspect that there are quite a few repeat audience members, perhaps introducing new friends to the experience.

After loud music and flashing lights that call the animated audience to attention, the five players enter the stage and stand in a line. To suggest period clothing, they are dressed in simple white lace-up cotton shirts, knee-length black breeches, high white or red stockings, and black leather shoes. One among them steps forward and explains, in the same words used for each performance, how their evening's proceedings work. He promises a full-length, never to be repeated, play following from an audience member's suggestion and then based on the "styles, themes, and language of Shakespeare."

Shakespeare's themes, and, often, whole story lines, were heavily influenced by the written Italian comedy and other written Italian sources, as were those of the commedia dell'arte. In an essay on the relationship between Shakespeare and his Italian sources, Louise George Clubb reminds us that "ransacking . . . [is] a first premise of Renaissance dramaturgy" including Shakespeare's (Clubb, 2002, p. 32). In addition to Shakespeare's familiarity with the unity of time, place, and action, his knowledge of the theory of genres and of pastoral structures and contents, all from Italian theatre, his use of "theatregrams of *topoi*, settings, characters, and encounters . . . proclaim the paternity of the long-cultivated and theorized Italian regular literary comedy as it was modified and transmitted in the style of professional troupes of the commedia dell'arte." His repeated use of these makes clear "the insistently Italianate character of much of Shakespeare's work" (Clubb, 2011, pp. 283, 285). Whether Shakespeare knew the Italian sources directly or not, he and they shared the same combinatory principles and the same repertory of theatregrams, that is, the same "units, figures, relationships, action, topoi, and framing patterns" (Clubb, 1986, p. 18).[9] Both Shakespeare and the commedia dell'arte composed their work by means of the interchange and transformation of these. The ISC has incorporated these same theatregrams and same method of composition into its work.

After telling the audience that tonight's performers will use the "styles, themes, and language of Shakespeare, the speaker continues "in case you are wondering how all this will turn out [pause], so are we." The audience laughs. In Chapter 1, I detailed the interest that improvisation in performance had for the audience. That interest is intensified in these performances before small audiences because an audience member has selected the title for it and because there is no prior scenario on which the improvisation is based. Truly no one, including the performers knows what will eventuate moment to moment.

The designated leader for the performance then calls for a moment of silence for Shakespeare, and with bowed heads the actors honor "the immortal Bard." The audience laughs uneasily. They will be offered something reminiscent of Shakespeare, but readily understood, and without the academic sanctity for Shakespeare that they have doubtless endured. This is Shakespeare light: fanciful, and often more athletic, rather like commedia.

Obeisance completed, the designated leader invites the audience to provide the title of the performance on which what they are about to see will be based. The first title the leader can make out in the din of suggestions is accepted by him and the actors repeat it. The rest of the cast exits while that leader presents a prologue consisting of a meditation on the title – in iambic lines, often rhymed, of varying lengths. The title for one recent performance was "He Walked into It." In an extended monolog the leader wondered what, in this case, "he" and "it" might mean. Sometimes titles do not seem very promising. "Hamlet: A Time Traveler's Dream" would seem, merely, to suggest a look back at *Hamlet*. Instead, in the performance, "hamlet" turned out to be a village called "Dogpatch" evoking both the cartoon Dick Tracy and Shakespeare's constable Dogberry. The language, characters, and action in the Improvised Shakespeare Company often manage, as here, to expresses something old and new at the same time. A performance with the title "The House of Trump" began immediately with a back-stabbing. When the occasion demands there are sexual double entendres, but more often the verbal double references are not obscene but work, like the action of the back-stabbing, both in the historical context and in reference to something today. Indeed, the audience members, as if to stump the players, are prone to provide titles with contemporary references that the actors are then obliged to make sense of in a Shakespearean context.

Throughout, actors enter the scenes, either from where they are sitting on the floor at the side of the playing area or from offstage. The first act, consists of three scenes followed by a group scene with all the actors, usually then performing lower-class characters, who together improvise a song or a game that both furthers the action and leaves the audience at a high point.

While the audience is served food and drink during the intermission between acts, the actors, backstage, review the names of the characters and their desires established to that point. They have used names from Shakespeare but freely attach them to characters of their own devising. In the second act, new characters may appear. But these are not discussed in the intermission. Discussion is entirely retrospective.

The second act, like the first, has three scenes, and a group scene that generally serves as the conclusion. The second act of "He Walked into It" began with a scene in which the old king explains to his scribe and confidant, that while, as established in the first act, he is officially giving up his throne to a son, he actually prefers that the scribe, who is not anyone who might logically be an heir to the throne, succeed him. The official coronation date has been set. The scribe agrees to ascend the throne and promises that, by dislodging a few critical building supports, he will see to it that during the arranged coronation, the building in which the coronation is to take place collapses on all those within. The king, satisfied with the plan, says that he is ailing and ready to die along with everyone else in the building.

The second act, second scene, begins with another game. In the commedia, it is what would be called a "*lazzi*," a gag. These, as in commedia, occur much more in performances by the Improvised Shakespeare Company than in Shakespeare. This one needs less contextualizing than does the one that ends the first act, so I provide it as an example. The scene has changed to the entryway of the coronation chamber. A seemingly endless stream of relatives, pretenders to the throne, and hangers-on explain to the scribe, who now serves as doorman, why they should be admitted. Each has a rationale more ludicrous than the previous one. Each actor enters and then reappears as yet another character seeking to enter. Naturally the scribe admits them all.

In the next scene, now in the coronation room, the coronation begins. Shortly afterward, the scribe has the building collapse as planned. In the ensuing melee, the scribe/doorman, just beyond the entrance to the coronation room, accidentally walks into a sword and dies. All who have walked into the coronation room die. A *deus ex machina*, a good queen, played by the person who initially contributed the prologue, mysteriously appears and provides the somewhat philosophical epilogue. Its last line, as a QED, like the title of every other performance, is the title of the show as it was initially provided by the audience member.

Company members have performed a densely plotted two-act comedy or, rather, tragicomedy with multiple characters much of it in various iambic meters, often rhymed. Not surprisingly ISC shows vary in quality from performer to performer and from show to show.

A brief sample of the group's work can be seen on YouTube at Improvised Shakespeare@Just for Laughs, from when they performed at the Just for Laughs Festival in Montreal Canada on July 23, 2010 (accessed July 20, 2019). As is their way, the ISC attempted to provide a complete play improvised on the spot on the basis of a title provided by an audience member. The anachronistic title supplied, "Rubber Crazy," would seem to have left little alternative but for something bawdy: the group of five men evidently had five minutes in which to perform. The performance began immediately: there was no moment of silence for Shakespeare, no prologue, no intermission, no epilogue. The stage had an upper balcony from which actors could enter, with stairs on which they could descend to stage level. Their spoken text follows:

"RUBBER CRAZY":

SUITOR (*at stage level*): Noble Celia, I wish to woo thee but why puts thou a barrier between us of contraception?

CELIA (also *at stage level*): For tis my will; I wish not to be laden with many a child. I wish to be free (*swirling and leaping about*) like that of the wind, the wind, the wind.

SUITOR: But noble maid, while I have spent three years fighting the wars, I have not visited another lady.

CELIA: Me thinks thou dost have a lie upon thy face.

FATHER (*entering, above*): And me thinks thou shoulds't have a sword about thy throat.

CELIA: Oh, Oh, gadzooks! Tis my father.

FATHER (*descending stairs*): Aye, left my daughter bereft of love and all happiness. Aye, a dark cloud has followed her ere thou hast left and now thou expecteth to be come back with opt arms?

SUITOR: Noble sir, I wish to do nothing but love thy daughter free of a cloak.

FATHER: I would hit thy jaw ere thou and my daughter would hit it raw.

SUITOR (*drawing sword*): Then sir, here be one sword that is not sheathed this night.

MOTHER (*above*): [played by Blaine Swen] Husband dost thou banish thy self from the comfort of our own bed?

SUITOR Have at thee, sir. (*Noisy duel between father and suitor*)

FATHER (*on floor, groaning*): I've been breamed [sic]. Aye, here in protection of my daughter's honor, in front of my own wife, I feel like I am now a goner.

MOTHER (*above*): Aye, indeed as my loins do burn for thee sweet husband, I beseech thee dispatch of this young buck and come to me for a randy . . . love-making session.

(Father *on floor, reaching for his sword*)

CELIA (*interceding between father and Suitor*): Nay, father, come do it not. I shall stand betwixt thee both, for I doth love this man. I would not have thee have him slain.

SUITOR: And thou hast shown me the wisdom of the rubber for now thou standeth between my sword and its aim. Come noble maid – a kiss, with my hand as guard.

CELIA: And I mine. (*They each put their hand before their mouth*)

CELIA (*changing her mind, lowers both her hand and that of the Suit*or): Nay – let us be raw about it. (*Actors, embarrassed, kiss)*

FRIAR (*enters at stage level, and speaks*): To it, youths. In sooth, aye, yonder friar peeped thee from yonder window. Thou dost thy romance grievous good. In sooth thou hast thought to put barriers 'twixt thy love and in o'er leaping them has found true love that might surpass all barriers placed between. (*Father gestures to mother to come down to stage level. FRIAR now addressing the daughter's parents*): Wouldst that thou could learn from their example.

FATHER: Aye, then we shall take up thy noble tactics and (*addressing youths*), if thou art married, thou might dispense of prophylactics.

SUITOR: Come the matter is . . . [indecipherable].

CELIA: Come let us take knee and heed thy call. (*Suitor and Celia kneel*)

FRIAR: Hold thy hands and gaze at thy wrists for ere that this play is over, I shall see thee both again tongue kiss. [*Much embarrassment between the actors playing the Suitor and Celia.*]

SUITOR: Tis only for these three to see. Tis not as if we're on T.V.

(*They tongue kiss to general rejoicing.*)

FRIAR: Aye, in they love never more be lazy, cast all aside and be no longer rubber crazy!

Several ideas – Celia's desire to be free of children, the suitor's faithfulness or lack thereof, the father's wound--are let drop. Perhaps in the urgency to present a complete play within the time-limit, the principle command of the Harold – "yes &," that is, working with whatever the previous actor has established – is not strictly obeyed. The general arc of the plot is clear: there is a beginning, with the suitor come home from the war set to reunite with his beloved; a conflict, established immediately between the girl's father and the suitor resulting in a swordfight between the girl's father and the suitor, and a resolution – the marriage of the suitor and the daughter. The characters and their relationships are familiar from Shakespeare and from commedia dell'arte. The theatregrams of the returning warrior, the conflict between the father and the daughter's suitor, the happy resolution in a marriage, are theatregrams Shakespeare and commedia have in common. The title of the play suggests to the actors, not protection of the girl's chastity, which would be the familiar theatregram, but from – perhaps today's equivalent – unprotected sex. The girl willingly gives up her freedom, including the freedom from having children. The implied homosexuality in the kisses and with it the audience's intensified awareness of the interplay between actor and role is familiar Shakespearian and commedia stuff. So are the sexual innuendoes. More than two actors expressing different points of view manage to improvise together, which a number scholars, have thought impossible (see Chapter 1, p. 11).

While the resulting language is nowhere near as dazzling as Shakespeare's, nor even Shakespearean, nor like what we can glean from the best of commedia, it nonetheless displays a rapid-fire linguistic virtuosity and verbal daring. Some of Louise George Clubb's words about a play by Giambattista della Porta (1535?–1615), influenced by *commedia erudite* as well as commedia dell'arte, do not seem entirely out of place in referring to ISC: "a rich macedoine of . . . city slang, . . . allusions, alliteration . . . hyperbolic parodies, and whizzing crosstalk – all perfectly artificial and perfectly natural to artificial characters in artificial surroundings" (1965, p. 146).

It is this linguistic virtuosity, with its blend of contemporary reference – T.V. and modern-day slang ("hit it raw" and "rubber") – Renaissance theatregrams and language at least suggestive of Shakespeare that audience have been coming back to for now thirteen years.

****

It is a myth that there is an unbroken line of commedia dell'arte continuing into the present day. However, a number of very long-lived troupes consciously continue to use aspects of commedia dell'arte performance resourcefully and successfully. The tradition is also honored, perhaps unwittingly, by a newer troupe in Chicago.

Notes

1 Filacanapa credits Giovanni Poli as one of the most important people in what he called the twentieth-century "reinvention" of commedia dell'arte. Filacanapa takes the cue for her essay from an unpublished 1962 post by him (Filacanapa, 2015, p. 379). Despite the title of her essay, "Giovanni Poli: The Missing Link," Filacanapa denies any continuity between what she calls neo-commedia dell'arte and *commedia dell'arte* (2018, pp. 379–380). Ironically, her essay is the penultimate one before the concluding section of the book, which, referring to commedia dell'arte, is entitled "Alive and well and living in. . . ." and consists of almost two hundred pages.

2 Signatories are Carlo Boso Luciano Brogi, Michele Casarin, Titino Carrara, Claudia Contin, Giancarlo Dettori, Antonio Fava, Ferruccio Marotti, Chistiano Roccamo, Serena Sartori, and Ferrucio Soleri (Balme, 2018, p. 313).

3 In 1985, Ferdinando Taviani referred to "the myth, entirely modern, of the commedia dell'arte" (Taviani, 1985, p. 124).
4 Campbell (2002, p. 20) explains that "Cynthia is another name for Diana, the goddess of the hunt, dedicated to chastity. The 'beloved youth' is Endymion, a shepherd whom Diana loved in her guise of goddess of the moon."
5 Campbell (2002 p. 21) explains that the "the Parcae (Fates) were the three powerful goddesses believed to preside over the life, death, and fortunes of each human being. . . . By declaring that she will become a Parca (Fate) to herself, Filli indicates that she will enact the part of [the Fate] Atropos by cutting her own life's thread, thus omitting suicide".
6 Copyright Arizona Board of Regents for Arizona State University. Reprinted with permission.
7 In 1972, Luis Valdez produced a film, "I Am Joaquin" based on Rodolfo Gonzalez's epic poem, a history of Chicanos, in effect, a call for unity and pride. The film reached many thousands of Chicanos (Huerta, 2006, pp. 246–247).
8 I would like to thank both Brendan Dowling and Blaine Swen of the ISC for the information they provided for this section.
9 Clubb coined the now widely accepted term "theatregram" in 1986 to explain the evident influence of the Italian theatre on Shakespeare, despite the fact that no one could point to direct influence. I have provided her original definition (1986, p. 18).

Works cited

Andreini, Francesco. ([1607] 1987). *Le bravure del Capitano Spavento.* Edited by Roberto Tessari. (Pisa: Giardini).

Andreini, Isabella. ([1588] 2002). *La Mirtilla: A Pastoral.* Translated with an introduction and notes by Julie D. Campbell. (Tempe: Arizona Center for Medieval and Renaissance Studies).

Andrews, Richard, ed. and trans. (2008). *The Commedia dell'Arte: A Translation and Analysis of 30 Scenarios of Flaminio Scala.* (Plymouth, UK: Scarecrow Press).

Balme, Christopher B. (2018). "Conclusion: *Commedia dell'Arte* and Cultural Heritage." In *Commedia dell'Arte in Context*, edited by Christopher B. Balme, Piermario Vescovo, and Daniele Vianello, pp. 311–319. (Cambridge: Cambridge University Press).

Campbell, Julie. (2002). Introduction. In *La Mirtilla: A Pastoral* by Isabella Andreini. Translated by Julie D. Campbell. (Tempe, AZ: Arizona Center for Medieval and Renaissance Studies).

Cixous, Hélène. (2016). *Politics, Ethics, and Performance: Hélène Cixous and the Théâtre du Solei.* Edited by Lara Stevens. (Melbourne, Australia: Re.Press).

Clubb, Louise George. (1965). *Giambattista Della Porta, Dramatist.* (Princeton, NJ: Princeton University Press).

Clubb, Louise George. (1986). "Theatregrams." In *Comparative Critical Approaches to Renaissance Comedy*, edited by Donald Beecher and Massimo Ciavolella, pp. 15–33. (Ottawa, Ontario, CAN: Dovehouse).

Clubb, Louise George. (2002). "Italian Stories on Stage." In *The Cambridge Companion to Shakespearean Comedy*, edited by Alexander Leggatt, pp. 32–46. (Cambridge: Cambridge University Press).

Clubb, Lousie George. (2011). "How Do We Know When Worlds Meet?" In *Shakespeare and Renaissance Literary Theories: Anglo-Italian Transactions*, edited by Michele Marrapodi, pp. 281–286. (Burlington, VT: Ashgate).

Doglio, Luisa Maria. (1995). *La Mirtilla.* (Lucca: Maria Pacini Fazzi)

Filacanapa, Giulia. (2015). "Giovanni Poli: The Missing Link." Translated by Eileen Cottis. In *The Routledge Companion to Commedia Dell'Arte*, edited by Judith Chaffee and Olly Crick, pp. 378–385. (London: Routledge).

Fisher-Lichte, Erika. (2018). "Staging Goldoni, Reinhardt, Strehler." In *Commedia dell'Arte in Context*, edited by Christopher B. Balme, Piermario Vescovo, and Daniele Vianello, pp. 266–276. (Cambridge: Cambridge University Press).

Guardenti, Renzo. (2018). "Iconography of the *Commedia dell'Arte*." In *Commedia dell'Arte in Context*, edited by Christopher B. Balme, Piermario Vescovo, and Daniele Vianello, pp. 208–226. (Cambridge: Cambridge University Press).

Hobsbawm, Eric, and Terence Ranger, eds. (1993). *The Invention of Tradition*. (Cambridge: Cambridge University Press).

Huerta, Jorge. (2006). "The Legacy of *El Campesino*." In *Restaging the Sixties: Radical Theaters and Their Legacies*, edited by James M. Harding and Cindy Rosenthal, pp. 239–261. (Ann Arbor: University of Michigan Press).

Huerta, Jorge. (2015). "The Legacy of Luis Valdez and El Teatro Campesino: The First Fifty Years [El Legado de Luis Valdez y El Teatro Campesino: Los Primeros Cincuenta Años]." Talk given at San Jose State University, September 24, 2015. howlround.com/the-legacy-of-luis-valdez-and-el-teatro-campesino (accessed 07-17-2018).

Katritzky, M.A. (2006). *The Art of Commedia: A Study in the Commedia dell'Arte 1560–1620 with Special Reference to the Visual Records*. (Amsterdam: Rodopi).

MacNeil, Anne. (2003). *Music and Women of the Commedia dell'Arte in the Late Sixteenth Century*. (Oxford: Oxford University Press).

Marrapodi, Michele. (2011). "The 'Woman as Wonder' Trope: From *Commedia Grave* to Shakespeare's *Pericles* and the Last Plays." In *Shakespeare and Renaissance Literary Theories: Anglo-Italian Transactions*, edited by Michele Marrapodi, pp. 175–202. (Burlington, VT: Ashgate).

Miller, Judith G. (2007). *Ariane Mnouchkine*. (London: Routledge).

Orenstein, Claudia. (2006). "Revolution Should Be Fun: A Critical Perspective on the San Francisco Mime Troupe." In *Restaging the Sixties: Radical Theaters and Their Legacies*, edited by James M. Harding and Cindy Rosenthal, pp. 175–195. (Ann Arbor: University of Michigan Press).

Pandolfi, Vito. (1957–1961). *La commedia dell'arte: storia e testi*. (6 vols). (Florence: Sansoni).

Schmitt, Natalie Crohn. (2014). *Befriending the Commedia dell'Arte of Flaminio Scala: The Comic Scenarios*. (Toronto, ON: University of Toronto Press).

Stevens, Lara. (2016) in Hélène Cixous, (2016). *Politics, Ethics, and Performance: Hélène Cixous and the Théâtre du Soliel*. Edited by Lara Stevens. (Melbourne, Australia: Re.Press).

Taviani, Ferdinando. (1985). "Positions du masque dans la commedia dell'arte." In *Le masque: du rite au théâtre*, edited by Odette Aslan and Denis Bablet, pp. 119–134. (Paris: Editions du Centre National de la Recherche Scientifique).

Vianello, Daniele. (2018). "Introduction to *Commedia dell'Arte*: History, Myth, Reception." In *Commedia dell'Arte in Context*, edited by Christopher B. Balme, Piermario Vescovo, and Daniele Vianello, pp. 1–14. (Cambridge: Cambridge University Press).

Wilbourne, Emily. (2016). *Seventeenth-Century Opera and the Sound of the Commedia dell'Arte*. (Chicago, IL: University of Chicago).

Wilmer, S.E. (2018). *Performing Statelessness in Europe*. (Bastingstoke, UK: Palgrave Macmillan).

Index

Note: Commedia dell'Arte characters are shown by the suffix [ch].

For Product Safety Concerns and Information please contact our EU representative GPSR@taylorandfrancis.com
Taylor & Francis Verlag GmbH, Kaufingerstraße 24, 80331 München, Germany

www.ingramcontent.com/pod-product-compliance
Lightning Source LLC
LaVergne TN
LVHW010613110826
845149LV00003B/895

* 9 7 8 1 0 3 2 0 8 8 5 0 1 *